"One of my favorite images when teaching world religions is the Mahayana Buddhist 'Jewel Net of Indra,' a web holding a multifaceted jewel at every node, each of which in turn reflects all the other gems of the mesh. In this book, Adam Tice has woven a 'Jewel Net of Advent.' The hymns, scriptures, reflective questions, and creative responses offer a dazzling webwork of ways to prepare for the coming of Christ."
—**MARY LOUISE BRINGLE**, professor of philosophy and religious studies at Brevard College and author of several hymn collections, including *In Wind and Wonder*

"This beautifully crafted and deeply thoughtful devotional invites us to encounter familiar hymns with fresh eyes and renewed spiritual depth. Tice's pastoral sensitivity and editorial care shine on every page as he draws out meaning with clarity, reverence, and insightful reminders of both the coming joy of heaven and the true presence of Christ already in our midst. Rooted in the hope that 'Christ may come to us now and always, and that we may have a song in our hearts to welcome him,' this work is a lasting companion for Advent, ensuring that our prayerful season of expectation is one we need never face alone."
—**KATE WILLIAMS**, vice president of Sacred Music at GIA Publications, Inc. and editor of *Gather—Fourth Edition*

"*Carols for the Coming Christ* offers wise words—but not too many!—which invite the reader into a space of reflection, inspiration, and refreshment. Tice has gifted us with an interactive tool enabling readers to go deep with the Christmas reality we treasure most by the music we love."
—**JAMES C. HOWELL**, pastor and author of multiple books, including *Heart of the Psalms* and *And His Name Shall Be Called: An Advent Devotional*

"*Carols for the Coming Christ* invites readers to slow down and truly inhabit the poetry, prayer, history, and theology of Advent and Christmas hymnody. The creative 'read, reflect, respond' approach transforms familiar carols into spaces for deeper spiritual listening, imagination, and meaningful engagement. These pages offer the same care, wisdom, and creativity Tice consistently brings to the church's song."
—**BEN BERGEY**, associate professor of music at Eastern Mennonite University and music editor for *Voices Together*

“A delightful invitation into the sacred songs of Advent and Christmas. The thoughtful pairing of hymn and biblical texts alongside insightful reflections gently nudges the reader to hear familiar words with new meaning. The daily response prompts encourage readers to explore their own creativity as they contemplate the deep gift of Emmanuel, God-with-Us.”
—**JOANNA HARADER**, author of *Prone to Wander* and *Expecting Emmanual*

“This book reminds us that the arts are not only woven into one holy and mystery-filled language; they also invite us to be more present in our very bodies and communities. What a blessing and a soul-touching challenge to have this collection edited by a serious poetry fan! It’s a delight to sit with songs curated for Advent that span so many centuries and styles, especially as Tice invites us to see the collection as a daily devotional: to rest in curiosity, read the lyrics aloud before singing, and respond through artistic prompts spanning drawing and movement to creative writing, Celtic spirituality, and theater. The five senses have a feast in this collection. It’s a wonderful new resource for worship and song leaders, as well as small group and families (Tice even suggests making notes in the margins of our personal hymnal copies, which I love!). We also gain fascinating insight into the fuller history of each carol and its creators.

During what can be an especially stressful and even painful season for those facing illness, infertility, or doubt, we are invited to let poetry and song take center stage in an Advent journey towards a Jesus who can love and transform us and our world, again and again. ‘What would you like to hear God sing?’ Tice asks. May we think of this beautiful, life-altering question every time we open a hymnbook, starting here.”
—**BECCA J. R. LACHMAN**, 2026–27 Poet Laureate of Athens, Ohio; writer and composer; and lyricist of “Could It Be That God Is Singing” (*Voices Together* 42)

CAROLS FOR THE COMING CHRIST

CAROLS FOR THE COMING CHRIST

A DAILY DEVOTIONAL FROM ADVENT TO EPIPHANY

ADAM M. L. TICE

HERALD PRESS
Harrisonburg, Virginia

Herald Press
PO Box 866, Harrisonburg, Virginia 22803
www.HeraldPress.com

Library of Congress Cataloging-in-Publication Data
Names: Tice, Adam M. L., 1979- author
Title: Carols for the coming Christ : a daily devotional from Advent to Epiphany / Adam M.L. Tice.
Description: Harrisonburg, Virginia : Herald Press, [2026] | Includes index.
Identifiers: LCCN 2026019502 (print) | LCCN 2026019503 (ebook) | ISBN 9781513817903 paperback | ISBN 9781513817910 epub
Subjects: LCSH: Advent | Christmas | Bible—Devotional use | Carols, English | Devotional literature | BISAC: RELIGION / Christian Living / Devotional | RELIGION / Christian Living / Spiritual Growth | LCGFT: Devotional literature | Meditations Classification: LCC BV40 .T524 2026 (print) | LCC BV40 (ebook)
LC record available at https://lccn.loc.gov/2026019502
LC ebook record available at https://lccn.loc.gov/2026019503

Study guides are available for many Herald Press titles at www.HeraldPress.com.

CAROLS FOR THE COMING CHRIST

Library of Congress Control Number: 2026019502
International Standard Book Number: 978-1-5138-1790-3 (paperback); 978-1-5138-1791-0 (ebook)
Cover and interior design by Merrill Miller
Printed in United States of America

30 29 28 27 26 10 9 8 7 6 5 4 3 2 1

Hark, the voice of one who's crying
in the desert far and near,
bidding all to full repentance,
since the kingdom now is here.
Oh, that warning cry obey!
Now prepare for God a way!
Valleys, rise in exaltation;
hills, bow down in adoration.

—Johannes Olearius, "Tröstet, tröstet, meine Lieben"

CONTENTS

DAILY REFLECTIONS

INTRODUCTION

Christmas would be virtually unrecognizable for many of us without carols. "O Come, O Come, Immanuel" sets the tone during Advent, and "Silent Night" sung by candlelight with wax precariously dripping is the sound of Christmas Eve. Public spaces and radio waves are saturated with Christmas music as soon as Halloween is over. The annual return of Mariah Carey's "All I Want for Christmas Is You," Boris Karloff intoning "You're a mean one, Mr. Grinch," and Vince Guaraldi's jazzy carol interpretations for *A Charlie Brown Christmas* pepper the secular soundscape.

Even as a musician, hymn writer, and music editor, I often find that the most familiar songs—those that I hear and sing over and over, year after year—still hold surprises. I can sing them almost too easily, without really taking the time to digest their message or appreciate their beauty. This book is an invitation to explore the songs of the season, familiar and new, and to discover how they can help us to welcome the incarnation of Jesus Christ, both as a newborn in Bethlehem and as God-with-us, here and now.

My approach is to experience these thirty-seven songs first and foremost as poetry. I invite you to dwell in the language of writers across centuries, from biblical times to the present day. Every generation has done its part to put into words the mystery of the Word made flesh. It may be self-serving to say this as a songwriter myself, but I think that the most appropriate medium for theology is poetry. Sung texts, carefully rendered in beautiful language but comprehensible enough to be memorized with just a few repetitions, are vehicles of faith formation. I would venture that much of what we think we know about many aspects of faith—including Christmas—owes more to the content of songs than to any other type of writing, perhaps including the Bible itself. In fact, much of Scripture itself is written as poetry and song, and much of what we sing in worship is drawn directly from Scripture. So let us take these poems seriously, examine what they have taught us, what they continue to teach, and perhaps what we have missed, despite deep familiarity.

Carols for the Coming Christ is structured as a daily devotional. If you begin on December 1 and complete one entry each day, you will finish on Epiphany, January 6. (In the church calendar, Advent officially starts the fourth Sunday before Christmas, which can fall anywhere between November 27 and December 3.) Each entry follows a pattern of "read, reflect, respond." Please resist the urge to start with singing! I encourage you to first read each song text in full—ideally, out loud. Appreciate the poetry and see what you notice. Your reading may become prayer.

A related scripture passage is included as well; meditate on the relationship between the hymn and the scripture. Many of the scriptures are presented in poetic form. The commentary that follows each song and scripture varies widely in content and scope, reflecting elements that I found interesting and fruitful for reflecting on the season. Some provide historical context; some delve into theology; some examine the structure of the poetry. My hope is that all will shed some new light on the texts under consideration and how they shape our Advent journey.

The *reflect* sections offer a question or two to ponder. These are generally open-ended and should not be construed as assuming there is a "right" answer. Feel free to follow whatever rabbit trails of thought or curiosity emerge.

The *respond* sections offer suggestions to creatively engage what you have encountered. Some involve writing or drawing; some are musical; some involve movement. My own creative work is most stimulated when I have some creative constraints. That is one of the appeals of traditional hymnody for me. Working within a set structure of rhyme and rhythm, with prescribed poetic line lengths, frees me to do my best writing. Some of the respond prompts include those kinds of constraints. They are intended to encourage creativity, but if they feel stifling or uninteresting, please find other avenues of artistic engagement. Choose your own medium for response; perhaps each entry will result in a sketch, or a haiku, or an interpretive movement, or your own new song. Let your imagination be your guide. Once you have read, reflected, and responded, by all means, sing the carol too!

On page 19 you will find a short guide for writing "hymnku." This is a framework that I use with songwriters to practice that craft. It is intended to be accessible to all levels of writers, from children to adults, beginners to experts. It may be an appealing option for responding to any of the devotional entries in either individual or group settings.

In addition to use as a daily devotional, the book could be used for small group study by focusing on a few songs at a time, reading aloud, and discussing the texts and reflection questions together. Groups could engage with the respond prompts either collectively or individually followed by sharing. I hope that this book will also be a useful resource for preachers and musicians as they plan and lead Advent and Christmas services. Several of the reflect and respond prompts could work well with children or for children's times during a service. I could also imagine choirs engaging the devotions together.

The selection of songs is most influenced by my work as text editor for the *Voices Together* (2020) hymnal. Every song included here can be found in that collection. In most cases the songs also appear in many other hymnals. A few of the more recent texts can be located on the websites of their respective copyright holders. I sought to reflect a variety of musical genres, cultural origins, and eras—though focusing almost exclusively on English-language material limits the degree of intercultural representation available for a book like this. Additionally, I hoped to include entries for a few songs from the contemporary worship music (CWM) genre, but licensing constraints limited what could be printed here. The omission of CWM texts should not be construed as a value judgment on musical styles. It is worth noting that very few seasonally specific songs have caught on in CWM, because even churches that exclusively rely on that musical language the rest of the year tend to return to "traditional" Christmas carols every December.

What is the difference between a *carol* and a *hymn*? There are historic definitions rooted in the origins and use of songs. Generally speaking, carols are considered to have originated in folk music traditions. Their design is often narrative, and they may feature culturally contextual elements from outside the biblical narrative. Hymns, in contrast, come from scholarly and literary roots and tend to dwell on theological points. The lines between those definitions may be interesting to hymnologists, but for the purposes of the average singer (or devotional book reader) they are generally not very important. Many songs blur the lines and do not fit neatly into one definition or the other. This book uses the terms interchangeably.

I determined the order of the songs around a few particular benchmarks. Several fixed dates—Christmas and Christmas Eve, in addition to Epiphany and winter solstice (for a "longest night" focus)—got particular selections. I grouped other texts around those dates according to the sequence of included scriptures. These scriptures are related in some way to the song texts. Many hymns are clearly connected to a particular biblical passage; some are even direct paraphrases. Others have looser thematic connections. Following the suggested sequence of hymns and scriptures in this devotional will take the reader on a journey through Advent, Christmas, and Epiphany.

Several subgroups of entries could be used as a shorter seasonal series, or may provide fodder for small groups:

December 1–9: Isaiah and other prophets longing for the Messiah

December 11–16: Luke's pre-nativity narratives, featuring Mary, Elizabeth, Zechariah, and John the Baptist

December 23–29: Matthew's version of the nativity

December 22, 30, 31, and January 1–3: Luke's version of the nativity

Several texts fall outside those broad categories as well, and these are interspersed between the larger groupings. Because the calendar dates and length of the liturgical season of Advent shift every year, I have not attempted to align the readings with any particular lectionary. A scripture text index with affiliated song titles is included in the back of the book.

A wealth of knowledge can be gleaned on any page of a hymnal. On page 17, you will find a guide to some of this information. Each text presented in this book includes ascription information as it would appear in a hymnal. From this you can see when and where the author lived and worked. I have also included the song's location within *Voices Together*, along with several other recent denominational hymnals when applicable. In some cases I have indicated texts that are related but not identical to what appears in this book. For example, another hymnal may use a different translation of the same source material. The hymnals are:

Glory to God (2013), Presbyterian Church USA

Evangelical Lutheran Worship (2006) and its supplement *All Creation Sings* (2020), Evangelical Lutheran Church in America and Evangelical Lutheran Church in Canada

Gather—Fourth Edition (2021), Roman Catholic

I have been singing some of these songs longer than I can remember. They have helped to form my faith and my understanding of the incarnation. Others are more recently written and provide new language to retell the familiar narrative or reinterpret it for our own age. And some I wrote myself. I began writing hymn texts over twenty years ago as a way of reflecting on what I believe. Because there were historically very few hymn text writers within my own Mennonite tradition, I hoped to provide language for worship that would reflect our particular ways of understanding what God is doing in the world. To my surprise I found that many other denominations were receptive to what I had to offer. That is indicative of the way that music (and the theology it carries) can transcend denominational differences.

I pray that this book will lead you into a greater appreciation for the role of songs in sustaining and shaping faith. I hope it will spark curiosity about the background and poetry of what you sing in worship beyond the thirty-seven found here. There is a wealth of information available. In preparing this book I relied on a few resources that I heartily recommend:

Hymnal Companion, Prepared by Churches in the Believers Church Tradition (1996) by Joan A. Fyock

Glory to God: A Companion (2016) by Carl P. Daw Jr.

The website Hymnary.org

The Canterbury Dictionary of Hymnology, available online at Hymnology.Hymnsam.co.uk (subscription required, but that is included in the price of membership in The Hymn Society, TheHymnSociety.org

May Christ come to us now and always, and may we have a song in our hearts to welcome him.

GUIDE TO A HYMNAL PAGE

A hymnal page contains a wealth of information. This example comes from *Voices Together.* The components may appear in different positions in other hymnals, but for the most part, the same elements will be present.

The heading at the top of the page is the thematic section of the hymnal in which the hymn is found. The numbers align with the songs rather than page numbers.

The title of the hymn is usually identical to the first line, although in some cases other phrases may be used.

Tunes and texts are named separately. This tune is named ST. LOUIS. Tune names are fully capitalized.

The textual meter of a hymn indicates the number of syllables in each line of poetry. If there are other texts or tunes with the same meter, they are often interchangeable. The meter is usually indicated numerically as here, but several standard hymn meters are listed with letters instead, such as CM, or common meter, which is 8.6.8.6 (eight syllables, then six, then eight and six again). Hymnals generally include indexes for titles / first lines, tunes, and meter. The metrical index can be used to mix and match texts and tunes. Sometimes a tune will require that syllables be squished together in order to fit the meter, so a word like *given*, normally two syllables, is rendered as *giv'n*, with the apostrophe indicating the omitted vowel.

Chords are provided for instrumentalists. As is the case of *Voices Together*, a separate accompaniment book may provide parts for piano or other instruments.

Songs often appear in four-part notation, for soprano, alto, tenor, and bass voices. The top (soprano) line is the melody, which can be sung by everyone if not singing in harmony. Many songs that are not written for harmony singing only include a melody line.

Hymn texts are divided into stanzas, each of which is sung to the same melody. This hymn has four stanzas. (The term *verse* is often used to mean the same thing. Sometimes *verse* is used if there is also a refrain or chorus, a section of the song that is typically sung at the end of every verse.)

The attribution lines include information about writers and composers, as well as translators and arrangers when applicable. They frequently include the date of composition and the title of the first publication to include the piece. *Voices Together* also lists the country or region and language of origin for non-English texts. The abbreviation alt. refers to an alteration of the source text. Copyright information may also be listed as relevant, with additional acknowledgments or rights information typically listed in the back of the hymnal.

HYMNKU:

An Exercise for Songwriting in Miniature

When I present workshops for aspiring songwriters, I frequently introduce a process for writing that I call "hymnku." Hymnku borrows its form from an Americanized version of traditional Japanese *haiku*; similarly, it consists of three lines. The first and third line are five syllables each, and the middle line is seven syllables. As an alternative to the suggested artistic responses in each devotional, readers might opt to create a daily hymnku instead.

In addition to the syllable count of each line, a hymnku follows a strict accent pattern, just like hymns. While informal English speech has varied patterns of accented syllables, traditional poetry and hymns use regular patterns. If multiple stanzas of a poem have the exact same accent pattern and number of syllables, they can be sung to a tune that shares the same pattern. Shakespeare used a pattern called *iambic* in much of his writing. Iambic lines begin on an unaccented syllable and alternate with accented syllables. "O Little Town of Bethlehem" is iambic. In the following line, read the capitalized syllables with a strong emphasis.

o LIT-tle TOWN of BETH-le-HEM, how STILL we SEE thee LIE.

Now try to read it with the other syllables emphasized:

O lit-TLE town OF beth-LE-hem, HOW still WE see THEE lie.

The opposite of iambic is *trochaic*, where the line begins with a strong syllable. Consider:

COME, thou LONG-ex-PEC-ted JE-sus.

I suggest writing a hymnku using a trochaic accent pattern:

STRONG weak STRONG weak STRONG
STRONG weak STRONG weak STRONG weak STRONG
STRONG weak STRONG weak STRONG

So, for example, here is a hymnku responding to "O Little Town of Bethlehem."

Tell us, Bethlehem,
were you really still that night?
Light comes streaming in.

If you are engaging these devotionals in a group setting, try writing hymnku collaboratively. Provide each person with a note card or piece of paper and have everyone write just one line of five syllables. Make sure the concept of the accent pattern is firmly established! Allow just a minute or two to write the line. Once it is written, writers should exchange their work, study what they have received, and then take a minute or two to add a second line (of seven syllables). Then pass the work to a third writer to add the final five-syllable line.

When I teach this process in workshops, I provide a simple tune to use as a framework. See if you can come up with a tune of your own once you have written a few hymnku.

DECEMBER 1

O come, O come, Immanuel,
and ransom captive Israel,
that mourns in lonely exile here,
until the Son of God appear.

Refrain:
Rejoice! Rejoice! Immanuel
shall come to thee, O Israel.

O come, O come, thou God of law,
in cloud and majesty and awe.
Thy precepts, taught on Sinai's height
call us to lives both just and right.
Refrain

O come, thou Rod of Jesse, free
thine own from Satan's tyranny.
From depths of hell thy people save,
and give them vict'ry o'er the grave.
Refrain

O come, thou Dayspring, come and cheer
our spirits by thine advent here.
Disperse the gloomy clouds of night,
and death's dark shadow put to flight.
Refrain

O come, thou Key of David, come
and open wide our heav'nly home.
Make safe the way that leads to thee
and close the path to misery.
Refrain

O come, thou Wisdom from on high,
and order all things far and nigh.
To us the path of knowledge show,
and cause us in thy ways to go.
Refrain

O come, Desire of nations, bind
all peoples in one heart and mind.
Bid envy, strife, and quarrels cease,
and fill the world with heaven's peace.
Refrain

Anonymous, *O Antiphons*, ca. 8th–9th c.; "Veni, veni Emmanuel," 12th c., stanzas 1–5 trans. John M. Neale (1818–1866, England), *Medieval Hymns and Sequences*, 1851, alt.; stanzas 6–7 trans. Henry Sloane Coffin (1877–1954, USA), *Hymns of the Kingdom of God*, 1916.

Voices Together 210, *Glory to God* 88, *Evangelical Lutheran Worship* 257, *Gather IV* 444

ISAIAH 11:1–5

A shoot will grow up from the stump of Jesse;
a branch will sprout from his roots.
The LORD's spirit will rest upon him,
a spirit of wisdom and understanding,
a spirit of planning and strength,
a spirit of knowledge and fear of the LORD.
He will delight in fearing the LORD.
He won't judge by appearances,
nor decide by hearsay.
He will judge the needy with righteousness,
and decide with equity for those who suffer in the land.
He will strike the violent with the rod of his mouth;
by the breath of his lips he will kill the wicked.
Righteousness will be the belt around his hips,
and faithfulness the belt around his waist.

Advent is a season of arrival and emergence. We anticipate the coming of the Messiah, the world's Savior, who will bring about God's dream for creation. What do we imagine this arrival will mean? "O Come, O Come, Immanuel" is a translation of "Veni, Veni, Immanuel," based on an ancient Latin text known as the *O Antiphons*, which ascribes seven titles to the coming Christ. In their original order they are:

Sapientia (Wisdom)
Adonai (Lord; here as "God of law")
Radix Jesse (Rod of Jesse)
Clavis David (Key of David)
Oriens (Dayspring)
Rex gentium (King of the nations; here as "Desire of nations")
Emmanuel / Immanuel (God-with-us)

Reading the first letters of these Latin titles in reverse, we have "Ero Cras"—"Tomorrow, I will come." The song was intended to be sung with one verse for each of the seven days leading up to Christmas Eve, with the seven titles culminating in one unified reality, fulfilling our Advent expectations in the person of Jesus. Several of these titles relate to the verses from Isaiah 11:1–5, which voices a longing for liberation. Yet even as the prophecy describes a powerful king, attributes like wisdom and understanding take priority.

REFLECT

A seven-stanza hymn with a refrain can feel awfully long, and song leaders will often pick and choose among their favorite portions. What aspects of Advent might be lost if some of the stanzas are omitted when singing this song text?

What three or four stanzas best describe the Messiah you anticipate this year?

Do any of the stanzas challenge your image of the Messiah?

RESPOND

"Rejoice! Rejoice! Immanuel / shall come to thee, O Israel." In this song, "Israel" refers not to the modern nation-state but to people who share a covenant with God. Immanuel comes to all people and all nations. Write a new version of this refrain that allows you to sing of a place, group, or individual whom you believe needs to experience the hope of God-with-us.

DECEMBER 2

Hope is a candle, once lit by the prophets,
never consumed, though it burns through the years;
dim in the daylight of power and priv'lege—
when they are gone, hope will shine on.

Peace is a candle to show us a pathway,
threatened by gusts from our rage and our greed.
Friend, feel no envy for those in the shadows—
violence and force their dead-end course.

Love is a candle whose light makes a circle,
where ev'ry face is the face of a friend.
Widen the circle by sharing and giving—
God's holy dare: love ev'rywhere.

Joy is a candle of mystery and laughter,
mystery of light that is born in the dark;
laughter at hearing the voice of an angel,
ever so near, casting out fear.

Christ is the light that the prophets awaited,
Christ is the lion, the lamb, and the child.
Christ is the love and the mystery and laughter—
candles, make way! Christ is the day.

Richard Leach (b. 1953, USA), 1994,
Voices Together 211

ISAIAH 60:1–3

Arise! Shine! Your light has come;
 the LORD's glory has shone upon you.
Though darkness covers the earth
 and gloom the nations,
 the LORD will shine upon you;
 God's glory will appear over you.
Nations will come to your light
 and kings to your dawning radiance.

This hymn includes a stanza for each of the themes associated with Advent Sundays and candles, though they do not quite follow the traditional order of hope, peace, joy, and love. The fifth stanza brings together all of the themes as signs pointing to Christ, the fulfillment of Advent expectation.

The first stanza describes candlelight as "dim in the daylight." Candles shine brightest in the darkness. In the Northern Hemisphere, Advent is experienced as a season of darkness, bringing particular resonance to images like these. The writer of this hymn avoids casting darkness as something dangerous or evil. In fact, he takes the opposite approach, treating it as a precondition for being able to perceive the coming light.

Isaiah 60 fully embraces the metaphor of light shining into the darkness, announcing the coming of a new day. In a modern age of electricity and artificial light, opportunities to experience darkness are few and far between. Our days are not as strictly defined by dawn and sunset, and it is easy to ignore the natural cycles of day and night. Being in the wilderness or away from lights in urban areas can deepen our appreciation for the subtle light of the moon and stars as well as the gradual changes that signal the coming dawn.

REFLECT

For those experiencing Advent in the Northern Hemisphere, how does the growing darkness shape your perspective on the season?

In the Southern Hemisphere, where days grow longer and lighter through the month of December, what different images and themes might take focus during Advent?

RESPOND

If you could add a Sunday to the Advent season, what would its theme be? What colors, symbols, scriptures, and songs would you want to experience on that Sunday?

DECEMBER 3

Comfort, comfort, O my people,
    speak of peace, now says our God.
Comfort those who sit in shadows,
    mourning 'neath their sorrows' load.
Speak unto Jerusalem
of the peace that waits for them.
    Tell of all the sins I cover,
    and that warfare now is over.

Hark, the voice of one who's crying
    in the desert far and near,
bidding all to full repentance,
    since the kingdom now is here.
Oh, that warning cry obey!
Now prepare for God a way!
    Valleys, rise in exaltation;
    hills, bow down in adoration.

O make straight what long was crooked,
    make the rougher places plain.
Let your hearts be true and humble,
    as befits a holy reign.
For the glory of our God
now o'er earth is shed abroad.
    And all flesh shall see the token
    that God's word is never broken.

Johannes Olearius (1611–1684, Germany), "Tröstet, tröstet, meine Lieben," *Geistliche Singe-Kunst*, 1671; trans. Catherine Winkworth (1827–1878, England), *Chorale Book for England*, 1863, alt.

Voices Together 212, *Glory to God* 87, *Evangelical Lutheran Worship* 256, *Gather IV* 466

ISAIAH 40:1–5

Comfort, comfort my people!
    says your God.
Speak compassionately to Jerusalem,
        and proclaim to her that her compulsory service has ended,
    that her penalty has been paid,
    that she has received from the LORD's hand double for all her sins!
A voice is crying out:
"Clear the LORD's way in the desert!
    Make a level highway in the wilderness for our God!
Every valley will be raised up,
    and every mountain and hill will be flattened.
    Uneven ground will become level,
    and rough terrain a valley plain.
The LORD's glory will appear,
    and all humanity will see it together;
    the LORD's mouth has commanded it."

The writer of Isaiah uses geographical metaphors to describe the condition of the world. Deep valleys, high hills, and crooked paths are all smoothed out to make way for the Messiah. In other Advent songs, we call upon God to come and redeem our brokenness. In this one, God calls upon us to prepare the world for Christ's coming. We are to speak comfort to those who suffer and to prepare a pathway for God. It is our responsibility to turn dangerous paths into safe and consistent roads.

Many of the song texts in this devotional paraphrase scripture. While a paraphrase is intended to make the source text singable (and thus memorable), the process is also one of interpretation. In this case, the translators move beyond the image of nature preparing the way for the arrival of God and apply the metaphor to spiritual preparedness as well, inviting people to "full repentance" and to be "true and humble."

REFLECT

What kind of metaphorical terrain would you use to describe the condition of the world today? What about your own community, family, or personal terrain?

In the first stanza we sing that "warfare now is over," yet that prophetic declaration is clearly not the reality of the world we know. What does it mean to proclaim peace when war seems never-ending?

RESPOND

Sketch a map of your current emotional terrain. What kind of pathway winds through it?

DECEMBER 4

Come, thou long-expected Jesus,
  born to set thy people free;
from our fears and sins release us,
  let us find our rest in thee:
Israel's strength and consolation,
  hope of all the earth thou art;
dear desire of ev'ry nation,
  joy of ev'ry longing heart.

Come, thou universal Savior;
  come, redeem the human race.
Life and joy spring from thy favor;
  cheer each soul in need of grace.
Still we wait for thine appearing—
  make our senseless struggles cease.
Guide us from our weary wand'ring
  into paths of perfect peace.

Born thy people to deliver,
  born a child, and yet a king;
born to reign in us forever,
  now thy gracious kingdom bring.
By thine own eternal Spirit,
  rule in all our hearts alone.
By thine all-sufficient merit,
  raise us to thy glorious throne.

Charles Wesley (1707–1788, England), *Hymns for the Nativity of Our Lord*, 1744; stanza 2 adapted from "Light of Those Whose Dreary Dwelling" in the same collection.

Voices Together 218, *Glory to God* 82 and 83, *Evangelical Lutheran Worship* 254, *Gather IV* 453

ISAIAH 9:2–3

The people walking in darkness have seen a great light.
On those living in a pitch-dark land, light has dawned.
You have made the nation great;
you have increased its joy.
They rejoiced before you as with joy at the harvest,
as those who divide plunder rejoice.

When the committee assembling *Voices Together* discussed this song text as found in the previous denominational hymnal, the only negative comment was that it should be longer. Knowing that Charles Wesley, a prolific writer, frequently wrote many more stanzas than are included in modern hymnals, we examined the source material. While we were surprised to find that Wesley did indeed write only two stanzas, the hymn that followed this one in the collection where it first appeared was in the same meter (8.7.8.7D) and included similar themes and phrases. We suspect Wesley may have written the two texts around the same time. The second text is not widely known and used today, but it interested us enough to adapt parts of it to become a new second stanza for "Come, Thou Long-Expected Jesus."

Once again, the arrival of light appears in the Isaiah passage as a metaphor for the dawn of peace for the people of Israel. Wesley's text also begins with Israel but recognizes Christ as the "desire of every nation" and as the path of peace for the universe, not just one particular group.

REFLECT

Does the coming of Jesus match our expectations? Are there ways in which Jesus' coming subverts expectations instead?

Does the added second stanza change how you experience the song as a whole?

RESPOND

Unlike many Christmas and Advent hymns, there is not a traditionally agreed upon tune pairing for this text. It is commonly sung to HYFRYDOL, STUTTGART (dividing each stanza in half), BEECHER, and JEFFERSON, among others. Using the Hymnary website or a hymnal's metrical index, try singing "Come, Thou Long-Expected Jesus" with another 8.7.8.7D tune.

For example, NETTLETON is a widely familiar tune commonly sung with "Come, Thou Fount of Every Blessing." Because it is the same textual meter, the tune can also be used for "Come, Thou Long-Expected Jesus." How does using a different melody impact the text?

DECEMBER 5

To us a child of hope is born,
to us a son is giv'n.
Him shall the tribes of earth obey,
him all the hosts of heav'n,
him shall the tribes of earth obey,
him all the hosts of heav'n.

His name shall be the Prince of peace,
forevermore adored,
the Wonderful, the Counselor,
the great and mighty Lord,
the Wonderful, the Counselor,
the great and mighty Lord.

His pow'r, increasing, still shall spread,
his reign no end shall know.
Justice shall guard his throne above,
and peace abound below,
justice shall guard his throne above,
and peace abound below.

Based on Isaiah 9:6–7; John Morison (1750–1798, Scotland), *Scottish Paraphrases*, 1781.
Voices Together 259

ISAIAH 9:4–7

As on the day of Midian, you've shattered the yoke
        that burdened them,
    the staff on their shoulders,
    and the rod of their oppressor.
Because every boot of the thundering warriors,
    and every garment rolled in blood
    will be burned, fuel for the fire.
A child is born to us, a son is given to us,
    and authority will be on his shoulders.
    He will be named
    Wonderful Counselor, Mighty God,
    Eternal Father, Prince of Peace.
There will be vast authority and endless peace
    for David's throne and for his kingdom,
    establishing and sustaining it
    with justice and righteousness
    now and forever.

The zeal of the LORD of heavenly forces will do this.

Because this hymn celebrates the arrival of the Messiah in the present tense, it is typically sung in the Christmas season, rather than during Advent's days of anticipation. The scripture it is drawn from, however, is still looking forward. Continuing the Isaiah 9 passage from yesterday's entry, the prophet proclaims the birth of the one who will deliver the people and bring peace. The cascade of titles may also be familiar from Handel's *Messiah*, where they are rendered as "Wonderful, Counselor, Almighty God, and Everlasting Father, the Prince of Peace."

John Morison's original text reflects more of the Isaiah passage, beginning with "The race that long in darkness pined." He even dared to include paraphrases of the challenging verses 4–5 (the first two sections of today's scripture):

> For thou our burden hast remov'd,
>   and quell'd th'oppressor's sway;
> Quick as the slaught'red squadrons fell
>   in Midian's evil day.
>
> Through shrieks of woe, and scenes of blood,
>   the warrior urges on;
> The lightning's speed, great Saviour! marks
>   the conquest thou hast won.

On their surface those lines stand in stark contrast to the desire for a Prince of Peace, and are generally omitted from contemporary hymnals. While it is likely best to not sing them in worship, their expression of hope for retributive violence is important to confront. In the context of Isaiah, the text voices the desire of an oppressed and exiled people who long for a release from captivity—and that vengeance is understood as God's purview and not something to be undertaken by the people. (The lines about Midian refer to Gideon and his three hundred men defeating a massive army in Judges 7, clearly regarded as a miracle of God's intervention.) Ultimately, it is the coming Christ who will rule with justice and peace.

REFLECT

Compare the scripture text to the hymn. What similarities and differences do you notice? What did Morison add or subtract in order to fit the constraints of hymn poetry? How do those decisions affect our understanding of the Isaiah text?

RESPOND

Write a prayer or a poem with sections addressed to Jesus using the titles listed in this hymn and scripture.

DECEMBER 6

We dream of a turning from ages of wrong,
earth to Eden restored, and our pardon.
Like Eve and Adam, join in a story and a song
as we wander with God through the garden.

Refrain:
Where true peace is shining as hate rolls away,
see, God's bright new creation is gleaming.
The morning rays that dawn on our weary, waking day
bring a hope far beyond all our dreaming.

We dream of a feast where there's no one outside,
turned away due to diff'rence or label,
when all the weapons forged to destroy or to divide
turn to rust far from God's holy table. *Refrain*

We dream of a mountain where no harm is done,
where the wolf and the lamb lie together.
A little child shall dance, leading all the creatures on,
as we join hand to hoof, claw, and feather! *Refrain*

Adam M. L. Tice (b. 1979, USA), 2008,
Voices Together 209

ISAIAH 11:6–9

The wolf will live with the lamb,
  and the leopard will lie down with the young goat;
  the calf and the young lion will feed together,
  and a little child will lead them.
The cow and the bear will graze.
  Their young will lie down together,
  and a lion will eat straw like an ox.
A nursing child will play over the snake's hole;
  toddlers will reach right over the serpent's den.
They won't harm or destroy anywhere on my holy mountain.
  The earth will surely be filled with the knowledge of the LORD,
  just as the water covers the sea.

Many parts of the Bible invite us to imagine a different reality than the one we experience. In Genesis we are presented with the story of the prototypical humans living in the garden of Eden and communing with God. In some ways the rest of the biblical story is about returning to that relationship—by repairing our connection to one another, to creation, and to God. Isaiah's delightful vision of the peaceable kingdom features animals normally seen as adversaries joining together with a little child to lead them. This text suggests that these kinds of visions are not only future hopes, but realities in the here and now, wherever "true peace is shining." They are a dream that comes true as we set aside hate and join in God's vision.

I wrote this song text with the classic Scottish tune LOCH LOMOND in mind. The tune has the capacity to be sung slowly with great longing, as well as quickly with great excitement. When I lead "We Dream of a Turning" I start quite slowly and get progressively faster with each verse. This allows singers to experience the vision of peace as both "not yet" and "already." We know the world is broken and aching, and we long for something better. God offers us glimpses of what yet will be, which we can celebrate here and now. Of all the texts I have written, the line "as we join hand to hoof, claw, and feather" remains one of my favorites.

REFLECT

What glimpses of hope do you see in the world today? Where is "true peace shining"?

In the context of Advent we can view the "little child" as Jesus. But why did Isaiah place a child among the wild animals? How do children help provide a vision of peace?

Have you ever had a dream that brought you a sense of hope or peace?

RESPOND

Sketch an unexpected pair of animals (any two *not* featured in Isaiah's vision) interacting as friends.

DECEMBER 7

Oh, how shall I receive thee,
how meet thee on thy way,
bless'd hope of ev'ry nation,
my soul's delight and stay?
O Jesus, Jesus, give me
now by thine own pure light
to know whate'er is pleasing
and welcome in thy sight.

Love caused thine incarnation;
Love brought thee here to me.
Thy thirst for my salvation
procured my liberty.
Oh, love beyond all telling,
that led thee to embrace,
in love, all loves excelling,
our troubled human race.

Thou comest, Christ, with gladness,
in mercy and good will,
to bring an end to sadness
and bid our fears be still.
We welcome thee, our Savior;
come gather us to thee,
that in thy light eternal
our joyous home may be.

Paul Gerhardt (1607–1676, present-day Germany), "Wie soll ich dich empfangen," *Praxis Pietatis Melica*, 1653; stanzas 1, 3, trans. Arthur T. Russell (1806–1874, England), *Psalms and Hymns*, 1851, alt.; stanza 2 *The Lutheran Hymnal*, 1941.

Voices Together 215, *Glory to God* 104, *Evangelical Lutheran Worship* 241

ISAIAH 61:1–4

The LORD God's spirit is upon me,
    because the LORD has anointed me.
He has sent me
    to bring good news to the poor,
    to bind up the brokenhearted,
    to proclaim release for captives,
        and liberation for prisoners,
    to proclaim the year of the LORD's favor
        and a day of vindication for our God,
    to comfort all who mourn,
    to provide for Zion's mourners,
    to give them a crown in place of ashes,
    oil of joy in place of mourning,
    a mantle of praise in place of discouragement.
They will be called Oaks of Righteousness,
    planted by the LORD to glorify himself.
They will rebuild the ancient ruins;
    they will restore formerly deserted places;
    they will renew ruined cities,
    places deserted in generations past.

The tune associated with this text is also used for a Palm Sunday hymn, "All Glory, Laud, and Honor." In fact, the original German text includes a stanza about the crowd waving palm branches when welcoming Jesus into Jerusalem one week before his crucifixion. Palm Sunday and the first Sunday in Advent share an emphasis on waiting for the arrival of Christ.

Hymn writer Paul Gerhardt suffered greatly during the Thirty Years' War (1618–1648), during which he lost his wife and four of their five children. His words reveal both gratitude for the incarnation and hope for an anticipated second coming when Christ will "bring an end to sadness."

What is it that we anticipate this Advent? As tomorrow's entry explores further, in the gospel of Luke, Jesus reads this scripture passage from Isaiah to describe what his mission will be. This is Jesus' own way of proclaiming his intentions. For Gerhardt, a survivor of war, Jesus offers healing, comfort, and joy. The writer sums this up with one word: *love*. It appears five times in the second stanza. It is the cause, motive, means, and end of Christ's coming to earth.

REFLECT

As the Gospels relate, the crowds who greeted Jesus on Palm Sunday turned away from him just a few days later. Is this another parallel with Advent? Are we excited to celebrate the arrival of a holy child, but less inclined to stay with him when things get difficult?

Paul Gerhardt lived through incredibly tumultuous times and responded with poetry that endures to this day. Where do you see people responding to the troubles of the world in creative and artistic ways today?

RESPOND

Love can be understood as a name for God in this hymn. Write a short prayer or poem addressed to God using the name Love. How does this shape the way you talk to God?

DECEMBER 8

Hark! the glad sound! The Savior comes!
  The Savior promised long!
Let ev'ry heart prepare a throne,
  and ev'ry voice a song.
On him the Spirit largely poured
  exerts its sacred fire,
wisdom and might, and zeal and love,
  his holy breast inspire.

He comes the pris'ners to release,
  in Satan's bondage held.
The gates of brass before him burst,
  the iron fetters yield.
He comes the broken heart to bind,
  the bleeding soul to cure,
and with the treasures of his grace
  to enrich the humble poor.

His silver trumpets publish loud
  the day of jubilee.
Our debts are all remitted now;
  he sets the people free.
Our glad hosannas, Prince of Peace,
  thy welcome shall proclaim,
and heav'n's eternal arches ring
  with thy beloved name.

Philip Doddridge (1702–1751, England), 1735, *Translation and Paraphrases*, 1745, alt.
Voices Together 217, *Evangelical Lutheran Worship* 239

LUKE 4:16–21

Jesus went to Nazareth, where he had been raised. On the Sabbath he went to the synagogue as he normally did and stood up to read. The synagogue assistant gave him the scroll from the prophet Isaiah. He unrolled the scroll and found the place where it was written:

The Spirit of the Lord is upon me,
because the Lord has anointed me.
He has sent me to preach good news to the poor,
to proclaim release to the prisoners
and recovery of sight to the blind,
to liberate the oppressed,
and to proclaim the year of the Lord's favor.

He rolled up the scroll, gave it back to the synagogue assistant, and sat down. Every eye in the synagogue was fixed on him. He began to explain to them, "Today, this scripture has been fulfilled just as you heard it."

Jubilee is an essential concept in the Bible. The books of Exodus and Leviticus describe how every seventh day was a *sabbath* set aside for rest from labor. Every seventh year was to be a *sabbatical* for the land, when agriculture was paused so that the land itself could rest. After forty-nine years (a cycle of seven sabbaticals) there was a jubilee year. This fiftieth year was intended as a time of debt forgiveness, release for enslaved people, and a return to ancestral lands for those displaced. In other words, jubilee leveled the economic and social playing field.

At the beginning of his ministry, when Jesus reads from Isaiah in the synagogue in his hometown, he identifies his work as an initiation of jubilee. Throughout his life, we witness how he carries out this proclamation. He heals the sick, feeds the hungry, uplifts the poor, and gives pride of place to the dispossessed. All of this is rooted in God's covenant. If we take Jesus' jubilee pronouncement seriously, then Advent should have economic and social implications. It can be tempting to understand these as separate from or in contrast to the spiritual significance of the coming of Christ, but our spiritual and physical realities are inextricably connected.

REFLECT

Do we find it easier to focus on spiritual concerns or social ones? In what ways is jubilee a spiritual aspiration? How might the spiritual dimensions of Advent invite us to a jubilee?

Compare today's scripture to its source in Isaiah (see yesterday's entry). Notice where Jesus stops his reading—at "the year of the Lord's favor." Is this significant? What does he add to the reading?

RESPOND

Imagine if one of the Sundays of Advent were devoted to the concept of jubilee. What symbolic or concrete actions could be included in worship? Write a call to worship or a sending blessing for a Sunday focused on jubilee.

DECEMBER 9

From the Parent's heart, the firstborn
when no worlds had been begun,
this is Alpha and Omega,
source and end that join as one
all that is now, ever has been,
and in future will be done,
evermore and evermore.

Word who ordered and created,
by whose word all came to be,
calling forth threefold creation:
heaven, earth, encircling sea,
filled with life that shares the moon's glow
and the sun's warm energy,
evermore and evermore.

Here is One whom seers and sages
longed to know in ancient days,
One foretold by faithful prophets,
singing with their hearts ablaze.
So shines forth the One long promised,
who inspires all creatures' praise,
evermore and evermore.

Let the highest heavens ring out
with angelic melody.
All who have the pow'r to praise God,
sing, wherever you may be.
Let no mortal tongue keep silent;
voices, blend in harmony,
evermore and evermore.

Aurelius Clemens Prudentius (348–ca. 410, present-day Spain), *Corde natus ex Parentis*, trans. Carl P. Daw Jr. (b. 1944, USA),

Voices Together 418; compare "Of the Father's Love Begotten" in *Glory to God* 108, *Evangelical Lutheran Worship* 295, *Gather IV* 483

HEBREWS 1:1–4

In the past, God spoke through the prophets to our ancestors in many times and many ways. In these final days, though, he spoke to us through a Son. God made his Son the heir of everything and created the world through him. The Son is the light of God's glory and the imprint of God's being. He maintains everything with his powerful message. After he carried out the cleansing of people from their sins, he sat down at the right side of the highest majesty. And the Son became so much greater than the other messengers, such as angels, that he received a more important title than theirs.

John Mason Neale and Henry W. Baker's widely sung translation of this early fifth-century text begins, "Of the Father's love begotten"—but intriguingly, the source text uses *parentis*, Latin for "parent's." Carl Daw's 2019 translation accounts for this and also delves deeply into the poetic artistry of Prudentius's text. Stanza 2 brings together scientific concepts with poetic imagery. In the beginning of Genesis, God first speaks light into existence. Modern physics regards energy as the fundamental building block of matter and of all reality. Drawing on the imagery of the moon's glow and the sun's warmth is not simply beautiful language; it links theology with physics.

The third stanza references the longing of seers, sages, and prophets for the coming of the Messiah. The passage from Hebrews also addresses the role of prophets, but it does not describe their work in terms of predicting the future. Biblical prophets spoke God's message for their own day. The Son comes as a fulfillment of their words in the sense that he continues their message, bringing (and being) the Word of God incarnate.

REFLECT

Just as songs can allow us to sing with people of different regions or cultures, they can also connect us to singers throughout history, joining in a tune that goes on "evermore and evermore." What can we learn from preserving and reimagining hymns like this one?

RESPOND

The tune associated with this text, DIVINUM MYSTERIUM, is often presented as a chant, with each syllable receiving roughly equal length. However, one of its first known printings, *Piae Cantiones* (1582), uses a 3/4 musical meter more typical of dance than sacred chant. The first note in most measures takes two beats; the second takes one. You can find this rhythm in the Episcopal *Hymnal 1982*. It can be found by searching on the Hymnary website.

Try singing the Daw translation both ways—with equal notes, and with the triple meter. What do you notice?

DECEMBER 10

"Sleepers, wake!" A voice astounds us.
The shout of rampart guards surrounds us:
    "Awake, Jerusalem, arise!"
Midnight's peace their cry has broken,
their urgent summons clearly spoken:
    "The time has come, O maidens wise!
Rise up, and give us light.
The Bridegroom is in sight. Alleluia!
Your lamps prepare and hasten there,
that you the wedding feast may share."

When we hear the heralds singing,
and in our hearts new joy is springing;
    we wake, and rise up from our gloom;
for our Friend comes down all-glorious,
the strong in grace, in truth victorious;
    our Star is risen, our Light is come!
Now come, O blessed One,
God's own beloved Son, Alleluia!
Oh, hear the call! Come one, come all,
and follow to the banquet hall!

All the heavens and earth adore you,
and saints and angels sing before you,
    with harp and cymbal's clearest tone;
gates of gleaming pearl before us
resound as angels sing in chorus
    and lead us to your dazzling throne.
No eye has seen that light,
no ear the echoed might of your glory;
but we rejoice and sing the song,
Alleluia! through ages long.

Philipp Nicolai (1556–1608, present-day Germany), "Wachet auf, ruft uns die Stimme," *Appendix to Freuden-Spiegel des ewigen Lebens*, 1599; stanza 1 trans. Carl P. Daw Jr. (b. 1944, USA); stanzas 2–3 trans. Catherine Winkworth (1827–1878, England), 1858; alt.

Voices Together 226, *Glory to God* 349, *Evangelical Lutheran Worship* 436

MATTHEW 25:1–13

At that time the kingdom of heaven will be like ten young bridesmaids who took their lamps and went out to meet the groom. Now five of them were wise, and the other five were foolish. The foolish ones took their lamps but didn't bring oil for them. But the wise ones took their lamps and also brought containers of oil.

When the groom was late in coming, they all became drowsy and went to sleep. But at midnight there was a cry, "Look, the groom! Come out to meet him."

Then all those bridesmaids got up and prepared their lamps. But the foolish bridesmaids said to the wise ones, "Give us some of your oil, because our lamps have gone out."

But the wise bridesmaids replied, "No, because if we share with you, there won't be enough for our lamps and yours. We have a better idea. You go to those who sell oil and buy some for yourselves." But while they were gone to buy oil, the groom came. Those who were ready went with him into the wedding. Then the door was shut.

Later the other bridesmaids came and said, "Lord, lord, open the door for us."

But he replied, "I tell you the truth, I don't know you."

Therefore, keep alert, because you don't know the day or the hour.

Philipp Nicolai was pastor of a Lutheran congregation that lost some thirteen hundred members to the bubonic plague. Nicolai sometimes buried thirty people a day. He wrote a book of meditations, including this hymn, as a reminder of his joy in Christ in the event of his own death, and as a comfort to those suffering from the disease themselves. Reading the hymn with that context lends a different perspective to Advent preparation. It entails another kind of "meeting Christ" altogether.

Despite this Matthew 25 scripture not appearing in the Revised Common Lectionary or the Roman Catholic Lectionary for the season of Advent, both the parable and this hymn are commonly associated with the season. Their themes may be best suited for the first Sunday of Advent because the readings focus on the second coming of Christ. In most Advent songs, we prepare ourselves and the world for Christ coming to us; in this one, we prepare for our own joyful entry into Christ's presence at the time of our death. Both cases entail an intersection between heaven and earth. With this perspective, we look not only to nativity, but to the return of Christ, or second coming—whatever form that may take. The concept of Christ's arrival among us is not a one-time historical event. Like the five wise women, we should always be prepared to welcome Christ into our midst.

REFLECT

How do you respond to Nicolai's call for joy even in the face of death? Does it feel inspirational or perhaps delusional?

How do the preparations of the five wise women inform or mirror our own spiritual preparation during Advent?

RESPOND

Johann Sebastian Bach (1685–1750) composed one of his most brilliant cantatas, "Wachet Auf," based on this German text. Many excellent recordings are available. Listen to it while drawing/doodling. See how long you can go without lifting your implement from the paper—just follow the flow of the music without trying to be representational. Decide whether you will cross your own lines or not. The full recording is around a half hour. If that feels too daunting, choose one movement. The first, fourth, and seventh movements are choral presentations of this text.

DECEMBER 11

Lo, how a Rose e'er blooming
    from tender stem has sprung!
Of Jesse's lineage coming
    as saints of old have sung.
It came, a flow'ret bright,
amid the cold of winter,
    when half spent was the night.

Isaiah 'twas foretold it,
    the Rose I have in mind.
With Mary we behold it,
    the virgin mother kind.
To show God's love aright,
she bore to us a Savior,
    when half spent was the night.

Flower, whose fragrance tender
    with sweetness fills the air,
dispel in glorious splendor
    gloom and grief ev'rywhere.
True man, yet very God,
from sin and death he saves us,
    and lightens ev'ry load.

Stanzas 1–2 anonymous, "Es ist ein Ros' entsprungen," *Alte Catholische Geistliche Kirchengasäng*, 1599; trans. Theodore Baker (1851–1934, USA), 1894; stanza 3 Friedrich Layritz (1808–1859, Germany), *Liederschatz*, 1832; trans. Harriet K. Spaeth (1845–1925, USA), *The Hymnal*, 1940, alt.

Voices Together 216, *Glory to God* 129, *Evangelical Lutheran Worship* 272, *Gather IV* 496

ISAIAH 7:14

Therefore, the Lord will give you a sign. The young woman is pregnant and is about to give birth to a son, and she will name him Immanuel.

While some metaphors for the coming Messiah evoke strength and monarchy, the image of a rose is decidedly tender, even fragile. The third stanza evokes the sense of smell—something not often included in hymns! We are, figuratively, invited to stop and smell the rose. It is this "fragrance" that will dispel "gloom and grief."

The original German text for this song likely refers to Mary as the blooming rose, but Protestant translations opted to orient singers to Jesus instead, referencing his mother as one with whom "we behold it." Since the time of the Reformation in the 1500s, Mary's status as one whom all generations will call "blessed" has often been downplayed or debated within Protestant circles. This was a reaction to the perceived overemphasis on her role in Catholic theology, but it also had the effect of diminishing the prominence of an essential biblical woman and, consequently, women in general within Protestant theology. The work of feminist theologians and hymn writers has equipped congregations to encounter Mary in new ways. She is not simply the "tender and mild" observer of the nativity, but a courageous young woman who said yes to God, taking on a central role in the story of our faith.

REFLECT

What scents do you associate with the seasons of Advent and Christmas? What memories do they bring to mind?

What does it mean to "behold" the coming of the Messiah with Mary? What does considering the story through her perspective teach us about Advent?

RESPOND

In the spirit of stopping to smell the roses, make a conscious effort to behold a few things today. Find opportunities to engage various senses as you do so: scent, sound, touch, taste, sight. Make a note of what you have beheld and consider how this kind of mindfulness shaped your day.

DECEMBER 12

God is here among us:
  come with adoration,
  fervent praise and expectation.
God is here within us:
  known beyond believing,
  soul in silent awe receiving.
God will name and will claim
  those beheld as lowly,
  making all things holy.

Come, abide within me;
  let my soul, like Mary,
  be thine earthly sanctuary.
Come, indwelling Spirit,
  with transfigured splendor;
  love and honor will I render.
Where I go here below,
  let me bow before thee,
  know thee, and adore thee.

Gladly we surrender
  earth's deceitful treasures,
  pride of life, and sinful pleasures.
God, we gladly offer
  thine to be forever,
  soul and life and each endeavor.
Thou alone shalt be known
  Lord of all our being,
  life's true way decreeing.

Gerhard Tersteegen (1695–1769, present-day Germany), "Gott ist gegenwärtig," *Geistliches Blumengärtlein*, 1729; trans. *The Hymnal*, 1940, alt.

Voices Together 62, *Glory to God* 412

LUKE 1:26–38

When Elizabeth was six months pregnant, God sent the angel Gabriel to Nazareth, a city in Galilee, to a virgin who was engaged to a man named Joseph, a descendant of David's house. The virgin's name was Mary. When the angel came to her, he said, "Rejoice, favored one! The Lord is with you!" She was confused by these words and wondered what kind of greeting this might be. The angel said, "Don't be afraid, Mary. God is honoring you. Look! You will conceive and give birth to a son, and you will name him Jesus. He will be great and he will be called the Son of the Most High. The Lord God will give him the throne of David his father. He will rule over Jacob's house forever, and there will be no end to his kingdom."

Then Mary said to the angel, "How will this happen since I haven't had sexual relations with a man?"

The angel replied, "The Holy Spirit will come over you and the power of the Most High will overshadow you. Therefore, the one who is to be born will be holy. He will be called God's Son. Look, even in her old age, your relative Elizabeth has conceived a son. This woman who was labeled 'unable to conceive' is now six months pregnant. Nothing is impossible for God."

Then Mary said, "I am the Lord's servant. Let it be with me just as you have said." Then the angel left her.

Many Advent songs have a wide scope, describing how society and nature will welcome the transformative reign of the coming Messiah. This hymn helps us turn inward and prepare for a personal transformation. Mary is upheld as a model for our faith, beginning with echoes of her Magnificat in Luke 1:46–55 in the lines "God will name . . . those beheld as lowly." (The entry for December 14 reflects further on this song from Mary.) In the second stanza, all of us, regardless of gender or ability to become pregnant, pray that we might be ready to become a sanctuary for Jesus, just as his mother was.

Mary's willingness to take on this role, as seen in the story from Luke, grew from initial fear, confusion, and questions. The angel Gabriel does not go find a more compliant potential mother or scold her for her questions; instead, he tells her how God will bring about the miraculous birth. Gabriel does not ask Mary a question or offer her a choice, but Mary responds to his pronouncement with agreement to God's plan.

The third stanza of the hymn outlines ways that we prepare ourselves—not in harsh, judgmental terms, but with gladness as we welcome Jesus as "Lord of all our being." Like Mary, we can bring fear, questions, and doubts, and still say, "Let it be with me just as you have said."

REFLECT

Does praying for societal change or for personal transformation come more naturally to you? What are the dangers of treating those prayers as distinct from each other?

RESPOND

Come up with a series of movements to go along with the song as you speak or sing it. Are there movements that feel right in the first stanza that you can also use for the second and third? Do you use a single gesture along with several lines of text? Or for an entire stanza? What parts of the song naturally suggest movements? What parts are more challenging?

DECEMBER 13

Unexpected and mysterious
  is the gentle Word of grace.
Ever loving and sustaining
  is the peace of God's embrace.
If we falter in our courage
  and we doubt what we have known,
God is faithful to console us
  as a mother tends her own.

In a momentary meeting
  of eternity and time,
Mary learned that she would carry
  both the mortal and divine.
Then she learned of God's compassion,
  of Elizabeth's great joy,
and she ran to greet the woman
  who would recognize her boy.

We are called to ponder mystery
  and await the coming Christ,
to embody God's compassion
  for each fragile human life.
God is with us in our longing
  to bring healing to the earth,
while we watch with joy and wonder
  for the promised Savior's birth.

Jeannette M. Lindholm (b. 1961, USA),
Voices Together 229, *Evangelical Lutheran Worship* 258

LUKE 1:39–45

Mary got up and hurried to a city in the Judean highlands. She entered Zechariah's home and greeted Elizabeth. When Elizabeth heard Mary's greeting, the child leaped in her womb, and Elizabeth was filled with the Holy Spirit. With a loud voice she blurted out, "God has blessed you above all women, and he has blessed the child you carry. Why do I have this honor, that the mother of my Lord should come to me? As soon as I heard your greeting, the baby in my womb jumped for joy. Happy is she who believed that the Lord would fulfill the promises he made to her."

In contrast to "Come, Thou Long-Expected Jesus" (see entry for December 4), this hymn focuses on the ways in which Jesus' arrival was "unexpected." The first stanza highlights that many experiences of grace are, in essence, unanticipated. By definition, they are outside the normal flow of life.

The only indication thus far that this is an Advent text is the subtle capitalization of "Word." The second stanza draws us into the story of Mary and her cousin Elizabeth, a character not often encountered in hymnody.

The moment of recognition when Elizabeth's baby "jumped for joy" is a dramatic foreshadowing of her son John the Baptist's role in announcing the arrival of the Messiah. The third stanza again turns to our own experience of the incarnation, here and now, as we "ponder mystery" and wait for Christ's coming. In keeping with a prophetic focus on justice, our experience of "God with us" is rooted in our hope for the healing of the earth and our participation in that healing.

REFLECT

What is the "momentary meeting / of eternity and time"?

Because they share a meter, this text can be sung to the same tunes used for "Come, Thou Long-Expected Jesus" (see the entry for December 4). Try singing it to one of those tunes. How does making that link affect the experience of this text? Does anything stand out to you compared to just reading the text or singing it to the tune it is paired with in a particular hymnal?

RESPOND

The song text calls us to "ponder mystery . . ." Choose a word or a phrase from this text to contemplate. Repeat it out loud. Write it down. See if it leads you in an unexpected direction—perhaps into a poem of your own.

DECEMBER 14

My soul cries out with a joyful shout
    that the God of my heart is great,
and my spirit sings of the wondrous things
    that you bring to the ones who wait.
You fixed your sight on your servant's plight,
    and my weakness you did not spurn,
so from east to west shall my name be blest.
    Could the world be about to turn?

Refrain:
My heart shall sing of the day you bring.
    Let the fires of your justice burn.
Wipe away all tears, for the dawn draws near,
    and the world is about to turn!

Though I am small, my God, my all,
    you work great things in me,
and your mercy will last from the depths of the past
    to the end of the age to be.
Your very name puts the proud to shame,
    and to those who would for you yearn,
you will show your might, put the strong to flight,
    for the world is about to turn. *Refrain*

From the halls of power to the fortress tower,
    not a stone will be left on stone.
Let the king beware for your justice tears
    ev'ry tyrant from his throne.
The hungry poor shall weep no more
    for the food they can never earn;
there are tables spread, ev'ry mouth be fed,
    for the world is about to turn. *Refrain*

Though the nations rage from age to age,
    we remember who holds us fast:
God's mercy must deliver us
    from the conqueror's crushing grasp.
This saving word that our forebears heard
    is the promise which holds us bound,
till the spear and rod can be crushed by God,
    who is turning the world around. *Refrain*

Voices Together 412, *Glory to God* 100, *Evangelical Lutheran Worship* 723, *Gather IV* 666

LUKE 1:46–55

Mary said,

"With all my heart I glorify the Lord!
    In the depths of who I am I rejoice in God my savior.
He has looked with favor on the low status of his servant.
    Look! From now on, everyone will consider me highly favored
        because the mighty one has done great things for me.

Holy is his name.
  He shows mercy to everyone,
    from one generation to the next,
    who honors him as God.
He has shown strength with his arm.
  He has scattered those with arrogant thoughts and proud inclinations.
  He has pulled the powerful down from their thrones
    and lifted up the lowly.
He has filled the hungry with good things
  and sent the rich away empty-handed.
He has come to the aid of his servant Israel,
    remembering his mercy,
  just as he promised to our ancestors,
    to Abraham and to Abraham's descendants forever."

Rory Cooney's paraphrase of Mary's Magnificat brings vigor to the radical text. His adaptation is incredibly memorable because of its use of frequent rhymes. These provide mental signposts through the wordy text, allowing singers to perceive it in smaller, interconnected units.

Mary's words, adapted from a poem sung by Hannah in 1 Samuel 2, describe a radical reshaping of the social order where the hungry are fed and the rich go away empty-handed. Mary (and Hannah before her) was keenly aware of the brokenness of the world. She lived under Roman occupation and would very soon become a target of King Herod's wrath. Even so, Mary understood that God's promises made to her ancestors would apply in her day as well. The wealthy and mighty would not have the final word. God would work through the humble and poor to do great things.

This song and "We Dream of a Turning" (see entry for December 6) both describe a coming turning of the world. Of course, the world is constantly spinning, and change is unrelenting. In the same way, the emergence of God's dream for the world is not simply a one-time event, but an ongoing incarnation where followers of Jesus continually grow more fully into his likeness.

REFLECT

Consider Mary's influence on Jesus as he grew. Did she teach him her song and others like it?

As with all scriptural paraphrases in song, there are similarities to and differences from the source text. What do you notice when you compare the song to the scripture text?

RESPOND

Mary's song is also a reminder to praise God not only for what God has done in the past, but also for what we anticipate God will do next. Write a short prayer for public worship that uses this approach.

DECEMBER 15

Bless'd be the God of Israel,
  who comes to set us free,
who visits and redeems us,
  and grants us liberty!
The prophets spoke of mercy,
  of freedom and release,
God shall fulfill the promise
  to bring our people peace.

Now from the house of David
  a child of grace is giv'n,
a Savior comes among us
  to raise us up to heav'n.
Before him goes the herald,
  forerunner in the way,
the prophet of salvation,
  the harbinger of day.

On all by death imprisoned
  the sun begins to rise,
the dawning of forgiveness
  upon the sinner's eyes,
to guide the feet of pilgrims
  along the paths of peace.
Oh, bless our God and Savior
  with songs that never cease!

Michael A. Perry (1942–1996, England), *Psalm Praise*, 1973, © 1973 Hope Publishing Co.
Voices Together 223, *Glory to God* 109, *Evangelical Lutheran Worship* 552

LUKE 1:67–79

John's father Zechariah was filled with the Holy Spirit and prophesied,

"Bless the Lord God of Israel
 because he has come to help and has delivered his people.
He has raised up a mighty savior for us in his servant David's house,
 just as he said through the mouths of his holy prophets long ago.
He has brought salvation from our enemies
 and from the power of all those who hate us.
He has shown the mercy promised to our ancestors,
 and remembered his holy covenant,
  the solemn pledge he made to our ancestor Abraham.
He has granted that we would be rescued
  from the power of our enemies
 so that we could serve him without fear,
  in holiness and righteousness in God's eyes,
  for as long as we live.
You, child, will be called a prophet of the Most High,
 for you will go before the Lord to prepare his way.
You will tell his people how to be saved
 through the forgiveness of their sins.
Because of our God's deep compassion,
 the dawn from heaven will break upon us,
 to give light to those who are sitting in darkness
 and in the shadow of death,
  to guide us on the path of peace."

In Luke 1:11–25, Gabriel visits Zechariah to tell him of Elizabeth's impending pregnancy with a son. Like Mary, Zechariah questions the angel, but in this case, Gabriel renders Zechariah unable to speak as a result of his unbelief. After John is born and his parents name him, Zechariah's voice returns, and he sings the hymn of praise recorded in this scripture passage. He celebrates not the end of his frustrating voicelessness, but the coming of the Messiah and his son John's role in preparing the way.

As with "O Come, O Come, Immanuel" (see the entry for December 1), naming "Israel" as the recipient of God's liberation does not refer to the modern nation; rather, Israel is a scriptural name for the people of God. The song is rooted in recounting God's faithfulness through history. Biblical prophets were not preoccupied with foretelling the future, but rather with proclaiming what the world could be and should become in light of God's promises.

REFLECT

Consider what it is like to recover an ability that was temporarily lost. For example, speaking again after laryngitis or resuming a sport after an injury. Does that recovery change the way you experience the ability?

RESPOND

The response for “Comfort, Comfort, O My People” (see the entry for December 3) invited you to draw a map of your emotional terrain. Draw another map of the “paths of peace” described in this hymn. How is this map similar to or different from that of your emotional geography?

DECEMBER 16

"Prepare the way!" the prophet called;
  a messenger will come
to reaffirm God's covenant
  and lead the people home.
The truth will shine like purest fire
  in that awaited hour.
Come, Jesus Christ! You are the way;
  renew us with your pow'r.

"Prepare the way!" cried John to all
  beside the Jordan stream.
All flesh will see God's saving work,
  the prophets' ancient dream.
The valleys and the mountaintops
  will make a level place.
Come, Jesus Christ! You are the way;
  restore us with your grace.

Prepare the way in us, O God,
  to greet that glorious day
when righteousness and peace will reign,
  and death will pass away.
The risen one will come again,
  descending from above.
Come, Jesus Christ! You are the way;
  redeem us with your love.

David Gambrell (b. 1972, USA), 2009,
Voices Together 220

LUKE 3:2B–6

God's word came to John son of Zechariah in the wilderness. John went throughout the region of the Jordan River, calling for people to be baptized to show that they were changing their hearts and lives and wanted God to forgive their sins. This is just as it was written in the scroll of the words of Isaiah the prophet,

A voice crying out in the wilderness:
"Prepare the way for the Lord;
make his paths straight.
Every valley will be filled,
and every mountain and hill will be leveled.
The crooked will be made straight
and the rough places made smooth.
All humanity will see God's salvation."

Some pastors and musicians are careful to wait until Christmas Day to start singing carols and nativity hymns. There is, after all, plenty to sing during Advent! One way to provide a taste of Christmas a bit early is to use traditional carol tunes paired with Advent-focused texts like this one. This song text, for example, is paired with the same tune used for "It Came Upon a Midnight Clear." As Luke 3 recounts, John the Baptist prepared the way for Jesus by instructing the wealthy to share with the poor and commanding the powerful to give up their exploitative ways. His calls for repentance went all the way to King Herod, which eventually led to John's execution.

The theme of preparation comes through in both the hymn and the scripture passage. The scripture quotes Isaiah 40:3–5, the same passage that inspired "Comfort, Comfort, O My People" (see the entry for December 3). Hymn writer David Gambrell directly identifies Jesus as the "way" foretold by both Isaiah and John.

REFLECT

How does singing this text with the tune associated with "It Came Upon a Midnight Clear" influence its meaning? Compare the two texts (see the entry for January 2). Are there common themes?

If John the Baptist were to prophesy in our own day, who might regard his words as a threat? How might he be received in your community or church?

RESPOND

Imagine composing a short note to an elected official or other leader of your choice in the style of John the Baptist. Consider adapting it into your own voice and style and actually sending it.

DECEMBER 17

Poor of the earth, I am a shepherd;
in rugged fields, I make my home.
Yet I attend the words of prophets,
and I can hope. How will I know?
Sprung from the roots, the line of Jesse,
will come one chosen for us all.
The prophet's songs foretell a leader—
a virgin's child. How will I know?

Another dawn, the sun before me,
another day to bide and watch.
I trust in God and I am waiting.
Day follows day. How will I know?
The nights are cold; I do not mind them,
my lambs rest safe within my care.
Companion moon is nightly changing;
my constant God: How will I know?

With each new day, I pause in wonder,
to look at Bethlehem afar.
From this small town will come a savior,
born in our midst. How will I know?
When time is right, God, share your purpose;
rulers and kings, they must be told.
I live apart. I wait in silence.
Who will tell me? How will I know?

This day is done, my prayers unanswered,
once more I sigh as darkness falls.
Your will be done, I must be patient;
I long for news. How will I know?
My bones are tired, my soul is hungry,
my stony bed awaits me now.
Do not forget your faithful shepherd.
Perhaps tonight. How will I know?

Jacque B. Jones (b. 1950, USA), 2011,
Voices Together 213

MICAH 5:2–5A

As for you, Bethlehem of Ephrathah,
though you are the least significant of Judah's forces,
one who is to be a ruler in Israel on my behalf will come out from you.
His origin is from remote times, from ancient days.
Therefore, he will give them up
until the time when she who is in labor gives birth.
The rest of his kin will return to the people of Israel.
He will stand and shepherd his flock in the strength of the LORD,
in the majesty of the name of the LORD his God.
They will dwell secure,
because he will surely become great throughout the earth;
he will become one of peace.

The writer of this text, Jacque Jones, has a background in theater, which informs her approach to narrative in her texts. Much like acting, voicing the words of another person invites us to encounter our similarities, differences, and assumptions in new ways.

With two thousand years of biblical interpretation behind us, it might seem easy to interpret ancient prophecies as pointing to the birth of Jesus. But how would shepherds tending flocks outside of Bethlehem interpret those same prophecies? Could they have anticipated that their hometown would play a central role in the coming of the Messiah?

The passage from Micah uses a shepherd as an image of how the coming ruler would care for his people. In Luke's gospel, the first people to hear of Jesus' arrival are shepherds, the "poor of the earth"—not unlike Jesus' inaugural sermon as an adult when he announces he has come to preach "good news to the poor" (Luke 4:18).

REFLECT

When the day-to-day concerns of life and work are foremost in our minds, how do we anticipate encountering God's work and presence in our world today?

What signs should we look for to understand what God is doing here and now?

RESPOND

Imagine a theatrical monologue for another character in the Advent/Christmas story. What questions would you ask if you were King Herod? Mary? The angel Gabriel? Elizabeth? One of the magi?

DECEMBER 18

He came down that we may have love;
he came down that we may have love;
he came down that we may have love;
  hallelujah for evermore.
Why did he come?

He came down that we may have peace;
he came down that we may have peace;
he came down that we may have peace;
  hallelujah for evermore.
Why did he come?

He came down that we may have joy;
he came down that we may have joy;
he came down that we may have joy;
  hallelujah for evermore.

Cameroon traditional.
Voices Together 239, *Glory to God* 137, *Evangelical Lutheran Worship* 253, *Gather IV* 486

1 JOHN 4:14–21

We have seen and testify that the Father has sent the Son to be the savior of the world. If any of us confess that Jesus is God's Son, God remains in us and we remain in God. We have known and have believed the love that God has for us.

God is love, and those who remain in love remain in God and God remains in them. This is how love has been perfected in us, so that we can have confidence on the Judgment Day, because we are exactly the same as God is in this world. There is no fear in love, but perfect love drives out fear, because fear expects punishment. The person who is afraid has not been made perfect in love. We love because God first loved us. Those who say, "I love God" and hate their brothers or sisters are liars. After all, those who don't love their brothers or sisters whom they have seen can hardly love God whom they have not seen! This commandment we have from him: Those who claim to love God ought to love their brother and sister also.

In much of sub-Saharan Africa, where this song originated, music and dance are inextricably linked. In many languages in the region, a single word is used for both. A congregation in these contexts would not sing while sitting still; movement would be required to embody the song.

Embodiment also describes how "the Word became flesh and made his home among us" (John 1:14). God became embodied so that we may have love, peace, and joy; and we can use our bodies to receive and share those good gifts. As the 1 John text reminds us, we continue to enact the incarnation by embodying God's love for one another. Love is embodied—it has hands and feet. By loving the people we "have seen," we make God tangible to them—and us. It is in experiencing love that we experience God. That is reason enough to sing . . . and dance!

REFLECT

"Why *did* he come?" This song provides a few answers, but theologians have written countless pages attempting to explain the purpose of the incarnation. How would you sum up the reason—or reasons—for the Word becoming human? What images, phrases, or explanations make sense to you?

RESPOND

Other single-syllable words can easily be substituted in the same position as *love* in the first stanza: light, life, hope, and so on. What other words might you sing? What if the phrase was "that we may *be* . . ." (instead of *have*)? What words would fit in that case?

What other combinations of phrases would you like to try?

that we may know . . .

that we may not . . .

that we may find . . .

DECEMBER 19

Now the heavens start to whisper,
    as the veil is growing thin.
Earth from slumber wakes to listen
    to the stirring, faint within:
seed of promise, deeply planted,
    child to spring from Jesse's stem!
Like the soil beneath the frostline,
    hearts grow soft to welcome him.

Heavy clouds that block the moonlight
    now begin to drift away.
Diamond brilliance through the darkness
    shines the hope of coming day.
Christ, the morning star of splendor,
    gleams within a world grown dim.
Heaven's ember fans to fullness;
    hearts grow warm to welcome him.

Christ, eternal sun of justice,
    Christ, the rose of wisdom's seed,
come to bless with fire and fragrance
    hours of yearning, hurt, and need.
In the lonely, in the stranger,
    in the outcast, hid from view:
child who comes to grace the manger,
    teach our hearts to welcome you.

Mary Louise Bringle (b. 1953, USA), 2005,

Voices Together 237, *Glory to God* 94, *All Creation Sings* 901

MATTHEW 25:37–40

Then those who are righteous will reply to him, "Lord, when did we see you hungry and feed you, or thirsty and give you a drink? When did we see you as a stranger and welcome you, or naked and give you clothes to wear? When did we see you sick or in prison and visit you?"

Then the king will reply to them, "I assure you that when you have done it for one of the least of these brothers and sisters of mine, you have done it for me."

Hymn writer Mary Louise Bringle was inspired by the Celtic concept of thin places, where the "veil" between heaven and earth is particularly permeable. Thin places may be locations or times when humans are better able to perceive God's movement and presence in the world. The island of Iona off the coast of Scotland is often described as a thin place. Pilgrims have traveled to visit the Iona Abbey for nearly fifteen hundred years, and the combination of history, a beautiful location, and an intentional structure of worship helps make the divine palpable.

The incarnation of Jesus is the ultimate intersection of heaven and earth—the point at which divinity becomes human—but all of creation bears the imprint of God's work. It is notable that after images of beauty and poetic explorations of the nativity, the hymn writer concludes that the most reliable place to experience the presence of Christ is among the poor and ignored among us. Here, she echoes Matthew 25, where we see that care for the poor, hungry, and thirsty is care for Jesus himself, thus demonstrating love and service is in itself a "thin place."

REFLECT

Are there physical locations, times, or occasions where you have experienced a greater awareness of God's presence, or a sense of unity between heaven and earth? Or do you experience something similar with certain people?

In what ways is a season like Advent a thin place? What might we do or practice in order to sharpen our perception of God's presence during this time of year?

RESPOND

Write a short call to worship that could follow this song. Include words of welcome for the people gathered as well as for Christ in the midst of the people.

DECEMBER 20

Let all mortal flesh keep silence,
  and with fear and trembling stand.
Ponder nothing earthly minded,
  for with blessing in his hand
Christ our God to earth descending
  comes, our homage to demand.

King of kings, yet born of Mary,
  as of old on earth he stood,
Lord of heaven now incarnate,
  in the body and the blood,
he will give to all the faithful
  his own self for heav'nly food.

Rank on rank the host of heaven
  streams before him on the way,
as the Light of light descending
  from the realms of endless day
comes, that pow'rs of hell may vanish,
  as the shadows pass away.

At his feet the six-winged seraph,
  cherubim with sleepless eye,
veil their faces to the Presence,
  as with ceaseless voice they cry,
"Alleluia! Alleluia!
  Alleluia, Lord Most High!"

From the Greek "Σιγησάτω πᾶσα σάρξ βροτεία," *Liturgy of St. James of Jerusalem* (Mediterranean), 5th c.; trans. Gerard Moultrie (1829–1885, England), *Lyra Eucharistica*, 2nd ed., 1864, alt.

Voices Together 65, *Glory to God* 347, *Evangelical Lutheran Worship* 490

ISAIAH 6:1–3

In the year of King Uzziah's death, I saw the Lord sitting on a high and exalted throne, the edges of his robe filling the temple. Winged creatures were stationed around him. Each had six wings: with two they veiled their faces, with two their feet, and with two they flew about. They shouted to each other, saying:

> "Holy, holy, holy is the LORD of heavenly forces!
> All the earth is filled with God's glory!"

While many of the Advent hymns explored in this book focused on the incarnation of the human Jesus, this one turns our perspective to the cosmic Christ—the one who is forever incarnate, forever human and divine, forever present and transcendent. This may be a helpful counterbalance to our tendency toward earthy cradle songs this time of year. The incarnation is a moment of transformation for all things. It is the dawn of God's new creation when "the pow'rs of hell . . . vanish." Even though Jesus arrived at one time and place, Christ remains incarnate in the world now. As the Isaiah 6 text recounts, "the earth is filled" with the glory of God, and that glory is present with us now.

The hymn identifies Christ as "now incarnate / in the body and the blood," which for the author particularly referenced the Eucharist, but the text can be interpreted more broadly without requiring discussion of doctrines like transubstantiation. Certainly communion is a time of awareness of Christ's presence. (Perhaps it qualifies as a *thin place*; see yesterday's reflection.) But even beyond that, Christ is present with us in "the body and the blood" of all who follow him. Each of us incarnates Christ in the world today when we love and serve as he did.

REFLECT

This hymn invites us to "ponder nothing earthly minded." What are some ways to experience this kind of contemplation? How does a cosmic perspective intersect with our genuine earthly concerns?

RESPOND

Isaiah 6 describes six-winged creatures known as seraphim. The cherubim and seraphim of the Bible are a far cry from the angels often depicted in art. Draw a seraphim as described in the Isaiah passage.

DECEMBER 21

Come now, O God, when our love is forsaken,
  come when our bedrock of faith has been shaken,
    come when our deepest of hopes are mistaken,
come, Emmanuel.
Come, Emmanuel.

Come when we squander the freedom you gave us,
  come, break the systems of sin that enslave us,
    come, though we wonder if you can still save us:
come, Emmanuel.
Come, Emmanuel.

Come, lead us out of our self-serving madness.
  Come, while the world is still shrouded in sadness,
    come, turn the tears of our mourning to gladness:
come, Emmanuel.
Come, Emmanuel.

David Bjorlin (b. 1984, USA),

Voices Together 143, *All Creation Sings* 902

ISAIAH 64:1–4

If only you would tear open the heavens and come down!
    Mountains would quake before you
    like fire igniting brushwood or making water boil.
If you would make your name known to your enemies,
    the nations would tremble in your presence.
When you accomplished wonders beyond all our expectations;
    when you came down, mountains quaked before you.
From ancient times,
    no one has heard,
    no ear has perceived,
    no eye has seen any god but you
    who acts on behalf of those who wait for him!

In the Northern Hemisphere, the longest night of the year falls a few days before Christmas. For many people, seasonal affective disorder, or SAD (brought on by the lack of sunlight), as well as the emotional baggage often associated with the holiday season, can mean that this time of year is more melancholy than merry. Many churches recognize this by offering a "longest night" or "blue Christmas" service, allowing worshipers to name their grief and bear their sorrows together. These services may also honor people who have lost loved ones during the year.

As Isaiah demonstrates, crying out to God with our anger and lament can be a deep expression of faith. Naming what we long for from within its absence proclaims what we believe is still possible by God's grace. David Bjorlin's text gives us language to articulate the "not yet" nature of Advent: We anticipate the coming of Emmanuel, but part of that anticipation is recognizing that the world is not currently what we expect it to become.

REFLECT

How can we support those who are experiencing grief and sorrow in our worship during Advent (and the rest of the year)?

How might you sing other Advent or Christmas songs in ways that make room for lament and grief? For example, imagine singing select verses from "O Come, O Come, Immanuel," but omitting the refrain or saving it to sing only at the very end.

RESPOND

Write (and send) a note of comfort and support to a friend or family member who is grieving.

DECEMBER 22

Spanish
Hacia Belén, se encamina
María con su amante esposo,
llevando en su compañía
a todo un Dios poderoso.

Estribillo:
Alegría, alegría, alegría,
Alegría, alegría y placer,
que la virgen va de paso
con su esposo hacia Belén.
Alegría, alegría, alegría,
Alegría, alegría y placer,
que la virgen va de paso
con su esposo hacia Belén.

Los pajarillos del bosque,
al ver pasar los esposos,
les cantaban melodías
con sus trinos armoniosos.

En cuanto a Belén llegaron
posada al punto pidieron,
nadie les quiso hospedar
porque tan pobres les vieron.

English
Mary journeyed with her husband
on the road to David's City.
She was bearing Christ our Savior,
only Son of God Almighty.

Refrain:
Alegrí, alegrí, alegría!
Oh, what joy and what gladness were there,
when the virgin and her husband
made their way to David's city.
Alegrí, alegrí, alegría!
Oh, what joy and what gladness were there,
when the virgin and her husband
made their way to Bethlehem.

From the forests, at their passing,
all the birds came swiftly winging,
as they watched this loving couple,
and burst into happy singing.

With the crowds in David's City,
not a single inn was able
to give shelter to the couple,
but a poor and lowly stable.

Voices Together 224, *Gather IV* 492

LUKE 2:1–7

In those days Caesar Augustus declared that everyone throughout the empire should be enrolled in the tax lists. This first enrollment occurred when Quirinius governed Syria. Everyone went to their own cities to be enrolled. Since Joseph belonged to David's house and family line, he went up from the city of Nazareth in Galilee to David's city, called Bethlehem, in Judea. He went to be enrolled together with Mary, who was promised to him in marriage and who was pregnant. While they were there, the time came for Mary to have her baby. She gave birth to her firstborn child, a son, wrapped him snugly, and laid him in a manger, because there was no place for them in the guestroom.

Las Posadas (Spanish for "the inns") is a traditional reenactment of Mary and Joseph's quest for room in Bethlehem prior to Jesus' birth. Celebrated in many Spanish-speaking communities, actors portraying the couple are accompanied by an entourage and a band as they go to various houses to request lodging. At the final location, Christmas carols are sung, food is shared, and piñatas are broken. This joyful song from Puerto Rico provides a narrative framework from within a Las Posadas tradition.

The fanciful verse about birds bursting into song might remind us that much of the way we picture the nativity is rooted in similarly fanciful, culturally rooted repetitions of the story. For example, there is no "innkeeper" recorded in Luke, and the types of livestock listed in various Christmas carols (like oxen and cattle) were more likely to be found in Victorian Europe than ancient Palestine. These elaborations on the story provide a sense of narrative familiarity and suggest that the Messiah can come anywhere, to anyone—not just in one time and place, but even here and now. As with Las Posadas, any home that we visit could be a home for Christ, and any guest we welcome could be Christ.

REFLECT

Sometimes it can be easier to identify culturally rooted but non-scriptural aspects of the Christmas story when they come from another culture. How can that knowledge help us when studying texts that emerge from within our own cultures? If you identify as part of a culture that does not use the kinds of songs explored in this devotional (which are largely rooted in American and European traditions), what images and themes stood out to you?

Imagine a Christmas pageant with modern-day characters set in your own community. Who would portray the holy family? What would they wear? What problems would they face? What animals would bear witness?

RESPOND

Find and learn about another Christmas carol from a culture or language different from your own. (Most hymnals include songs from a number of cultures in their Christmas sections.) What images surprise you?

DECEMBER 23

Come, join in Mary's prophet-song
　　of justice for the earth,
for right outgrows the fiercest wrong,
　　revealing human worth—
bound not within the wealth we crave
　　or in the arms we bear,
but in the holy sign God gave:
　　the image that we share.

The "Peace on earth" which shepherds heard
　　is not some fantasy.
The angels sang to greet the Word,
　　whose birth is victory.
The maiden Mary, not so mild,
　　bore into death's domain
true God, and yet an infant child,
　　who over death would reign.

Emmanuel, God-with-us here,
　　grows peace where we would dare
to act despite our trembling fear
　　and bring God's holy care.
The image God made "us" to be
　　is also borne on "them."
Christ bids us join our enemy
　　to sing war's requiem.

Adam M. L. Tice (b. 1979, USA), 2005,
Voices Together 246

MATTHEW 1:18–25

This is how the birth of Jesus Christ took place. When Mary his mother was engaged to Joseph, before they were married, she became pregnant by the Holy Spirit. Joseph her husband was a righteous man. Because he didn't want to humiliate her, he decided to call off their engagement quietly. As he was thinking about this, an angel from the Lord appeared to him in a dream and said, "Joseph son of David, don't be afraid to take Mary as your wife, because the child she carries was conceived by the Holy Spirit. She will give birth to a son, and you will call him Jesus, because he will save his people from their sins." Now all of this took place so that what the Lord had spoken through the prophet would be fulfilled:

> *Look! A virgin will become pregnant and give birth to a son,*
> *And they will call him,* Emmanuel.

(*Emmanuel* means "God with us.")

When Joseph woke up, he did just as an angel from God commanded and took Mary as his wife. But he didn't have sexual relations with her until she gave birth to a son. Joseph called him Jesus.

I wrote this hymn text in December 2005 when four members of Christian Peacemaker Teams (now Community Peacemaker Teams, or CPT) were being held hostage during the war in Iraq. They were in the country pursuing peace after the US invasion in 2003. Tom Fox, a Quaker activist, was killed, and the other three were eventually freed.

I was inspired by their courage, and it occurred to me that, like Mary, they sought to bear God into the domain of death. Writing this text was my way of praying for peace in the midst of conflict. The trappings of the season were on my mind and entered the text—shepherds and angels, and courageous Mary—but it felt like they were contending with the violent realities of our world. The CPT hostages insisted on nonviolent responses to war because they valued every human life. One way of experiencing the presence of Emmanuel is to remember that the image of God is present in every human. Every face we see, enemy or friend, reveals God-with-us.

REFLECT

In contrast to many Christmas carols, this hymn refers to Mary as "not so mild." What other traditional images or descriptions of Christmas could use a bit of tweaking?

The words *bear*, *bore*, or *borne* appear in the sixth line of each stanza. How do the ideas in those lines connect?

RESPOND

Using magazines, catalogs, newspapers, or old photographs, create an "image of God" collage.

CHRISTMAS EVE

Silent night, holy night!
All is calm, all is bright
round yon virgin mother and child!
Holy infant, so tender and mild,
sleep in heavenly peace,
sleep in heavenly peace.

Silent night, holy night!
Shepherds quake at the sight:
glories stream from heaven afar,
heav'nly hosts sing, "Alleluia!
Christ the Savior is born,
Christ the Savior is born!"

Silent night, holy night!
Son of God, love's pure light,
radiant, beams from thy holy face
with the dawn of redeeming grace,
Jesus, Lord, at thy birth,
Jesus, Lord, at thy birth!

Silent night, holy night!
Wondrous star, lend thy light.
With the angels let us sing
"Alleluia" to our King,
"Christ the Savior is born,
Christ the Savior is born."

"Stille nacht, heilige nacht," Joseph Mohr (1792–1848, Austria), 1817, *Leipziger Gesangbuch*, 1838; English trans. John F. Young (1820–1885, USA), *The Sunday School Service and Tune Book*, 1863

Voices Together 244, *Glory to God* 122, *Evangelical Lutheran Worship* 281, *Gather IV* 476

MATTHEW 2:1–2

After Jesus was born in Bethlehem in the territory of Judea during the rule of King Herod, magi came from the east to Jerusalem. They asked, "Where is the newborn king of the Jews? We've seen his star in the east, and we've come to honor him."

This poem was written by Austrian pastor Joseph Mohr in 1816. Franz Xavier Gruber wrote the tune the following year, and it was first sung on Christmas Eve, 1818. According to tradition, the organ in Mohr's church was broken, so singing was accompanied by guitar. The song quickly gained regional popularity and within a decade was introduced in the United States by touring folk singers. It has become so ubiquitous across languages and cultures that, for many people, it is a defining element of the Christmas season.

Like many Christmas carols and hymns, "Silent Night" integrates material from both the Luke and Matthew nativity stories. For instance, the star of Bethlehem is integral to Matthew's version, guiding the magi, or "wise men," to Bethlehem. It is not mentioned in the Luke narrative. A song like this is not made to present a systematic theological argument or to paraphrase a biblical narrative. Instead, it provides images for meditation and adoration. It invites us to place ourselves within the scenes, beholding the wondrous birth.

REFLECT

What traditions do you associate with singing "Silent Night"?

Stanza 3 can be difficult to parse from hearing alone. Note that *beams* is a verb here, not a noun. With that in mind, what is stanza 3 saying?

RESPOND

Sketch a nativity scene. Include yourself in the drawing. Where are you? What position are you in?

CHRISTMAS DAY

O little town of Bethlehem,
how still we see thee lie!
Above thy deep and dreamless sleep
the silent stars go by.
Yet in thy dark streets shineth
the everlasting light;
the hopes and fears of all the years
are met in thee tonight.

For Christ is born of Mary,
and gathered all above,
while mortals sleep, the angels keep
their watch of wond'ring love.
O morning stars, together
proclaim the holy birth!
And praises sing—let "Glory!" ring
with peace to all on earth!

How silently, how silently,
the wondrous gift is giv'n!
So God imparts to human hearts
the blessings of the heav'ns.
No ear may hear his coming,
but in this world of sin,
where meek souls will receive him still
the dear Christ enters in.

O holy Child of Bethlehem,
descend to us, we pray,
cast out our sin, and enter in,
be born in us today!
We hear the Christmas angels
the great glad tidings tell.
O come to us, abide with us,
our Lord Emmanuel.

Phillips Brooks (1835–1893, USA), 1868, *Sunday School Services and Hymn Book*, 1870, alt.
Voices Together 245, *Glory to God* 121, *Evangelical Lutheran Worship* 279, *Gather IV* 482

MATTHEW 2:3–6

When King Herod heard this, he was troubled, and everyone in Jerusalem was troubled with him. He gathered all the chief priests and the legal experts and asked them where the Christ was to be born. They said, "In Bethlehem of Judea, for this is what the prophet wrote:

You, Bethlehem, land of Judah,
by no means are you least among the rulers of Judah,
because from you will come one who governs,
who will shepherd my people Israel."

Emmanuel: God is with us. Heaven is inextricably linked with earth via humanity. God became embodied and came to dwell among us. God's plan of redemption for creation is not achieved by an army of angels that swoops in and enforces God's will. Instead, the realm of God grows in one tiny human body, with and for all of us. The army of angels shows up, but not for a fight: They assemble to sing "Glory!"

This is still how God shows up among us. Not in terror and thunder, but in solidarity with humanity. To "meek souls who receive him still . . . Christ enters in." Phillips Brooks's original text includes a stanza omitted from most modern hymnals. Part of it follows:

> . . . where charity stands watching
> and faith holds wide the door,
> the dark night wakes, the glory breaks,
> and Christmas comes once more.

As with a number of songs we have encountered, Brooks recognized that the continued enactment of peace among people, especially the poor and neglected, is fundamental to sharing Christ's ongoing presence in the world.

REFLECT

Bethlehem is in the modern-day West Bank, a part of Palestine controlled by the State of Israel. Decades of conflict have made contemporary Bethlehem a far cry from the silent streets imagined in this carol. How does it feel to sing about imagined peace in the midst of real-world suffering? How do carols provide us with a different vision of what the world could (or ought to) be?

RESPOND

Christmas Day can often be a chaotic, noisy time of gathering and celebration. There may not be many moments to ponder "how silently the wondrous gift is given." Instead, listen for sounds that give you joy today, especially those that surprise you. Make a list of what you hear, and see if it becomes a poem or inspires other artwork.

DECEMBER 26

Where is this stupendous Stranger?
    Prophets, shepherds, kings, advise!
Lead me to my Master's manger,
    show me where my Savior lies.

O most Mighty, O most Holy,
    far beyond the seraph's thought,
are you then so mean and lowly
    as unheeded prophets taught?

Oh, the magnitude of meekness!
    worth from worth immortal sprung!
Oh, the strength of infant weakness,
    if eternal is so young!

God all bounteous, all creative,
    whom our sins could not dissuade,
you have come to be a native
    of the very world you made.

Christopher Smart (1722–1771, England), *Hymns and Spiritual Songs . . .*, 1765, alt.
Voices Together 266

MATTHEW 2:7–8

Then Herod secretly called for the magi and found out from them the time when the star had first appeared. He sent them to Bethlehem, saying, "Go and search carefully for the child. When you've found him, report to me so that I too may go and honor him."

Christopher Smart is largely forgotten as a hymn writer, despite his mastery as a poet. He is now primarily remembered for his *Jubilate Agno* (Latin for "Rejoice in the Lamb"), parts of which were set to music by Benjamin Britten, including a portion which begins, "For I will consider my cat, Jeoffrey." He spent years of his adult life in debtors' prisons and insane asylums. Smart's poetry is marked by fanciful imagery, as well as obscure language. This is one of the stanzas not included in hymnals:

Spinks and ouzels sing sublimely,
  "We too have a Saviour born;"
Whiter blossoms burst untimely
  On the blest Mosaic thorn.

While the language is sonically delightful, its meaning is virtually incomprehensible to modern ears. "Spinks" are sparrows; "ouzels" are blackbirds. The last two lines reference a legend related to Joseph of Arimathea, who arranged for Jesus' burial after the crucifixion. The four stanzas included in the modern hymn text are themselves updated. Among other changes, the second line in the original referenced "Swains of Solyma," meaning "Shepherds of Jerusalem." The hymn as revised remains strikingly beautiful and poetic, highlighting the paradox of the incarnation.

The intentions of those seeking the place of Jesus' birth were mixed. The magi sought to witness the fulfillment of prophecy, whereas King Herod had nefarious motives. The Matthew nativity story emphasizes that Jesus' birth was a threat to existing power structures. Herod was right to regard the incarnation as a challenge to his authority, but the nature of that threat was beyond his understanding. Instead of another power-hungry king, Jesus came in the "strength of infant weakness."

REFLECT

How might the hymn writer's experience of poverty and mental illness have influenced his understanding of the incarnation?

What elements of paradox do you see in the text?

RESPOND

In honor of Christopher Smart's affection for animals, write a story or poem or draw a picture in honor of an animal associated with the nativity (whether mentioned in the Bible or not!)

DECEMBER 27

Hail the bless'd morn, see the great Mediator
    down from the region of glory descend!
Shepherds, go worship the babe in the manger;
    lo, for his guard the bright angels attend.

Shall we not yield him, in costly devotion,
    fragrance of Edom and off'rings divine,
gems of the mountain and pearls of the ocean,
    myrrh from the forest or gold from the mine?

Vainly we offer each ample oblation,
    vainly with gifts would his favor secure.
Richer by far is the heart's adoration,
    dearer to God are the pray'rs of the poor.

Cold on his cradle the dewdrops are shining,
    low lies his head with the beasts of the stall.
Angels adore him in slumber reclining,
    Maker and Monarch and Savior of all.

Brightest and best of the stars of the morning,
    dawn on our darkness and lend us thine aid.
Star of the East, the horizon adorning,
    guide where our infant Redeemer is laid.

Stanza 1 anonymous; stanzas 2–5 Reginald Heber (1783–1826, England), *Christian Observer*, 1811, alt.

Voices Together 272, *Evangelical Lutheran Worship* 303

MATTHEW 2:9–10

When they heard the king, they went; and look, the star they had seen in the east went ahead of them until it stood over the place where the child was. When they saw the star, they were filled with joy.

Some hymns are so laden with obscure vocabulary and complex syntax that it may take multiple readings (and a dictionary) to fully interpret the meaning. This is especially true when focused on singing, as some of our concentration is applied to the music, leaving less for the words. In addition, the way that words are divided into syllables in the musical score adds an additional obstacle. Consider:

am - ple ob - la - tion

But as with the works of Shakespeare, taking some extra time to appreciate the poetry of a text can help aid both comprehension and appreciation. In this case, the flowery language flows out like a rich offering—itself an "ample oblation." The writer Reginald Heber uses these extravagant images to illustrate his point. The richest of gifts, described in ornate language, pale in comparison to something he presents in the simplest, most direct line of the text: "dearer to God are the pray'rs of the poor." The line includes only a single multisyllabic word (*dearer*). The rest of the line is one word per note of music, making it direct, simple, and comprehensible, much like what it describes.

The visit of the magi recorded in Matthew is a fascinating aspect of the nativity story. Who were they: sages, astrologers, mystics? Why did they study prophecies about a coming Jewish king if they were not themselves Jewish? One enduring interpretation is that their presence in the story signals that Jesus' birth was an incarnation not just for one people or nation, but for all people.

REFLECT

Find the line in the hymn that consists of only single-syllable words. What does this line have in common with the "dearer" line discussed earlier?

RESPOND

Write a prayer or a short poem (perhaps in hymnku form—see p. 19) using only single-syllable words.

DECEMBER 28

What child is this, who, laid to rest,
    on Mary's lap is sleeping,
whom angels greet with anthems sweet,
    while shepherds watch are keeping?
This, this is Christ the King,
whom shepherds guard and angels sing.
Haste, haste to bring him laud,
the babe, the son of Mary!

Why lies he in such mean estate
    where ox and ass are feeding?
Good Christian, fear, for sinners here
    the silent Word is pleading.
Nails, spear shall pierce him through,
the cross be borne for me, for you.
Hail, hail the Word-made-flesh,
the babe, the son of Mary!

So bring him incense, gold, and myrrh;
    come, peasant, king, to own him.
The King of kings salvation brings;
    let loving hearts enthrone him.
Raise, raise the song on high;
the virgin sings her lullaby.
Joy, joy, for Christ is born,
the babe, the son of Mary!

William C. Dix (1837–1898, England), *Christmas Carols New and Old*, 1871.
Voices Together 267, *Glory to God* 145, *Evangelical Lutheran Worship* 296, *Gather IV* 508

MATTHEW 2:11–12

They entered the house and saw the child with Mary his mother. Falling to their knees, they honored him. Then they opened their treasure chests and presented him with gifts of gold, frankincense, and myrrh. Because they were warned in a dream not to return to Herod, they went back to their own country by another route.

Although William Dix was a fairly prolific hymn writer, his two most widely published texts in modern hymnals both happen to deal with the visit of the magi to Jesus' family after his birth. One is the text presented here; the other is "As with Gladness Men of Old." His approach to the narrative, while still gilded with Victorian-era images of an English nativity, compares favorably to the popular "We Three Kings," which takes more substantial liberties with the story.

A compelling element of this text is the reminder of the brutal reality of incarnation: By becoming human, Jesus would also face death. "Nails, spear shall pierce him through," and the cross awaits. There are various interpretations about the meaning of the three gifts presented to Jesus—to symbolize his kingship, divinity, and humanity; to represent his role as priest and intercessor; to foreshadow his death and burial. An online search for "gold, frankincense, and myrrh" will provide ample fodder for research.

REFLECT

The Matthew nativity account does not tell us how long after Jesus' birth the magi arrived. There is nothing to indicate that they crowded around the manger along with the shepherds, ox, ass, sheep, Mary, Joseph, and a little drummer boy. Yet this tableau continues to dominate carols, Christmas pageants, and popular media. Does it matter whether popular nativity imagery reflects the biblical narrative?

In several contemporary hymnals, this hymn is sung simultaneously with another one titled "Helpless and Hungry" (also known as "Child of the Poor"). Find a recording of the two paired together. How does the newer text change how you experience "What Child Is This"?

RESPOND

If Jesus were born in our own time, what gifts might be modern equivalents to those brought by the magi? Write a three-part poem, with two lines devoted to each of your suggested gifts.

DECEMBER 29

Jesus entered Egypt
    fleeing Herod's hand,
living as an alien
    in a foreign land.
Far from home and country
    with his family,
was there room and welcome
    for this refugee?

Jesus was a migrant
    living as a guest
with the friends and strangers
    who could offer rest.
Do we hold wealth lightly
    so that we can share
shelter with the homeless,
    and abundant care?

Jesus crosses borders
    with the wand'ring poor,
searching for a refuge,
    for an open door.
Do our words and actions
    answer Jesus' plea,
"Give the lowly welcome,
    and you welcome me"?

Adam M. L. Tice (b. 1979, USA), 2007,
Voices Together 279, *Glory to God* 154

MATTHEW 2:13–16

When the magi had departed, an angel from the Lord appeared to Joseph in a dream and said, "Get up. Take the child and his mother and escape to Egypt. Stay there until I tell you, for Herod will soon search for the child in order to kill him." Joseph got up and, during the night, took the child and his mother to Egypt. He stayed there until Herod died. This fulfilled what the Lord had spoken through the prophet: *I have called my son out of Egypt*.

When Herod knew the magi had fooled him, he grew very angry. He sent soldiers to kill all the children in Bethlehem and in all the surrounding territory who were two years old and younger, according to the time that he had learned from the magi.

Amid the joy of the holiday season, it can be tempting to gloss over or ignore the story that follows Jesus' birth in Matthew. Jesus and his family flee from Herod's violence and live as refugees in Egypt. Like "Now the Heavens Start to Whisper" (see entry for December 19), this song text concludes with an allusion to Matthew 25:31–46, the parable in which Jesus links our salvation to our treatment of "the least of these"—people in need of comfort, food, and water.

In our own day, refugees are displaced worldwide. After fleeing from horrific circumstances, they are often met with hostility, suspicion, and xenophobia. Following a Christ who crosses borders means welcoming those seeking safety and rest, because Christ is present in them.

REFLECT

How do you think his family's experience as refugees influenced Jesus' life and ministry?

Each stanza of this hymn ends with a question. How might you answer those questions personally? Or on behalf of your congregation, community, or nation?

RESPOND

Write a short prayer for use in public worship. Address it to the God who was once a refugee.

DECEMBER 30

In the beginning was the Word,
no other sound in heaven heard. Alleluia!
There at the dawning of all things,
one wondrous word creation sings: Alleluia!

One Word, that gave all others birth,
dwelled with the God of all the earth. Alleluia!
One Word, one Wisdom so divine,
one holy wholeness God's design. Alleluia!

Thus, all that is began to be,
born of this perfect unity. Alleluia!
All that has life and breath was stirred,
sung into being by the Word. Alleluia!

Among us came this Word to dwell,
the Word made flesh, Emmanuel! Alleluia!
Though in our sin we failed to see,
still by this Word we are set free. Alleluia!

Still shining in the deepest night,
no shadow can put out the light. Alleluia!
Let all that is within us praise
God's Word of grace and truth always! Alleluia!

Chris Shelton (b. 1978, USA),
Voices Together 270

JOHN 1:1–5

In the beginning was the Word
    and the Word was with God
    and the Word was God.
The Word was with God in the beginning.
Everything came into being through the Word,
    and without the Word
    nothing came into being.
What came into being
    through the Word was life,
    and the life was the light for all people.
The light shines in the darkness,
    and the darkness doesn't extinguish the light.

While the authors of Luke and Matthew describe the coming of Christ with narrative, John begins with poetry. This meditation on the incarnate Word dwelling with humanity, the Word that "was with God" and "was God," paradoxically uses words to describe a mystery beyond words. How else but poetry to approach such transcendence?

In ancient times, any public proclamation was likely chanted or sung in order to be heard across a wide area. Thus when we read in Genesis 1 that God said, "Let there be light," it is reasonable to imagine God *singing* creation into being rather than simply speaking. Along with the songs of Mary and Zechariah found in Luke (see the entries for December 14 and 15), it is especially appropriate to sing this scripture passage, not just read it. In this hymn of scriptural paraphrase, writer Chris Shelton intersperses an appropriate response to the mysterious text: "Alleluia!"

REFLECT

How does singing rather than speaking change the significance of a proclamation? What would you like to hear God sing?

What difference does it make to use poetry to explore theology? How does this John 1 passage differ from other approaches, like a sermon or a story?

RESPOND

Write a poem inspired by this scripture, using "Word" at the beginning of every line.

NEW YEAR'S EVE

While shepherds watched their flocks by night,
all seated on the ground,
the angel of the Lord came down,
and glory shone around.

"Fear not," said he, for mighty dread
had seized their troubled mind.
"Glad tidings of great joy I bring
to you and humankind.

"To you, in David's town, this day
is born of David's line
the Savior, who is Christ the Lord,
and this shall be the sign:

"The heav'nly babe you there shall find
to human view displayed,
all humbly wrapped in swathing bands,
and in a manger laid."

The angel spoke, and suddenly
appeared a shining throng
of angels praising God, and thus
addressed their joyful song:

"All glory be to God on high
and to the earth be peace,
goodwill henceforth from heav'n to earth
begin and never cease!"

Nahum Tate (1652–1715, England), 1700, alt.
Voices Together 253, *Glory to God* 117 and 118, *All Creation Sings* 913

LUKE 2:8–9

Nearby shepherds were living in the fields, guarding their sheep at night. The Lord's angel stood before them, the Lord's glory shone around them, and they were terrified.

Prior to this text, nearly every English-language song for worship was a psalm rendered in poetic meter. Nahum Tate's foray into the New Testament followed the same approach, paraphrasing the narrative from the King James Bible into singable verse, making it the very first Christmas hymn published in English. (There were many "folk" Christmas carols prior to this, but they were not approved for use in worship.)

Like contemporary hymn writer Jacque Jones (see the December 17 entry on "Poor of the Earth"), Tate had a background in theater. In fact, his best-known work outside of hymnody was a version of Shakespeare's *King Lear* revised to provide a happy ending. His affinity for drama shines through in his use of action language.

Christmas pageants are deeply rooted in the history of Christian worship. They provided a way of presenting the biblical narrative that was accessible to all, regardless of ability to read. Additionally, in the case of pre-Reformation worship, services were conducted exclusively in Latin and would have been unintelligible to most people. Like stained glass windows that visually present Bible stories, dramas were essential teaching tools. Unsurprisingly, narrative verse remains a popular form for Christmas hymns. They provide a memorable way of introducing and reinforcing the story.

REFLECT

What would Christmas be without the songs we expect to sing year after year? Imagine a time before Christmas hymns were an integral part of worship.

Imagine that you are totally unfamiliar with the Christmas story. If you heard or saw it presented for the very first time, what would you find surprising?

RESPOND

Act out this hymn, using the narrative parts as stage directions.

NEW YEAR'S DAY

From heav'n above to earth I come
to bear good news to ev'ryone.
Glad tidings of great joy I bring
to all the world, and gladly sing:

To you a child is come this morn,
of Mary, chosen maiden, born.
This little child, of lowly birth,
shall be the joy of all the earth.

This is the Christ, God's Son most high,
who hears your sad and bitter cry.
He will himself your Savior be
and from all sin will set you free.

Welcome to earth, O noble Guest,
through whom this sinful world is bless'd!
You turned not from our needs away!
How can our thanks such love repay?

My heart for very joy now leaps.
My voice no longer silence keeps.
I, too, must join the angel throng
to sing with joy his cradle song.

"Glory to God in highest heav'n,
who unto us a Son has giv'n."
With angels sing in joyful mirth
a glad new year to all the earth!

Martin Luther (1483–1546, present-day Germany), *Geistliche Lieder*, 1535; trans. Catherine Winkworth (1827–1878, England), *Lyra Germanica*, Series 1, 1855; trans. composite Inter-Lutheran Commission on Worship, alt., ; portions of stanzas 2, 4 George MacDonald (1824–1905, Scotland), *Exotics*, 1876.

Voices Together 263, *Glory to God* 111, *Evangelical Lutheran Worship* 268

LUKE 2:10–12

The angel said, "Don't be afraid! Look! I bring good news to you—wonderful, joyous news for all people. Your savior is born today in David's city. He is Christ the Lord. This is a sign for you: you will find a newborn baby wrapped snugly and lying in a manger."

Each angel appearance in the first two chapters of Luke includes the phrase "Don't be afraid!" This stands in contrast to the Matthew nativity, where angelic messages are conveyed in dreams. What was it about the angels that caused fear? Here and with Zechariah (Luke 1:13), "Don't be afraid" are the angel's very first words. But with Mary (Luke 1:28–30), the angel's blessing and greeting come first. "Don't be afraid" comes only after she is confused by his words. Perhaps Zechariah and the shepherds were more startled by the appearance of a stranger in an unexpected place—inside the temple in Zechariah's case, and out in the fields at night for the shepherds.

Reformer Martin Luther wrote this hymn for his children and used it as a miniature Christmas Eve pageant at home. (Luther had six children; two did not reach adulthood.) The opening stanzas were sung by someone dressed as an angel, with the children responding to the angel's pronouncements. Luther was an advocate for children's education. This was integral to his emphasis on scriptural literacy. *Sola scriptura*, or scripture alone, was one of the key components of his reforms. He taught that all people should be empowered to engage with scripture. In Saxony, the region of Germany where Luther lived, it was customary at the time to mark the arrival of the New Year at Christmas rather than January 1, hence the final line of the text: "A glad new year to all the earth!"

REFLECT

The "voice" in this hymn changes at various points. Who is the speaker, and who is being addressed in each stanza? How might you present this song in a way that makes those shifts clear?

RESPOND

Write a new stanza to bring an additional character into the story, drawing inspiration from either the Matthew or Luke narratives—perhaps Mary or Joseph greeting the shepherds, or King Herod hearing rumors of a new king's arrival.

JANUARY 2

It came upon a midnight clear,
that glorious song of old,
from angels bending near the earth
to touch their harps of gold:
"Peace on the earth, good will to all
from heaven's gracious King."
The world in solemn stillness lay,
to hear the angels sing.

Still through the cloven skies they come,
with peaceful wings unfurled,
and still their heav'nly music floats
o'er all the weary world.
Above its sad and lowly plains
they bend on hov'ring wing,
and ever o'er its Babel sounds
the blessed angels sing.

Yet with the woes of sin and strife,
the world has suffered long;
beneath the heav'nly hymn have rolled
two thousand years of wrong,
and warring humankind hears not
the tidings which they bring.
O hush the noise and cease your strife
and hear the angels sing.

And you, beneath life's crushing load,
whose forms are bending low,
who toil along the climbing way
with painful steps and slow:
Look now! for glad and golden hours
come swiftly on the wing.
O rest beside the weary road,
and hear the angels sing.

For lo, the days are hast'ning on,
by prophet bards foretold,
when, with the ever-circling years
comes round the age of gold,
when peace shall over all the earth
its ancient splendors fling,
and all the world sends back the song
which now the angels sing.

Edmund H. Sears (1810–1876, USA), *Christian Register*, 1849, alt.

Voices Together 248, *Glory to God* 123, *Evangelical Lutheran Worship* 282, *Gather IV* 470

LUKE 2:13–14

Suddenly a great assembly of the heavenly forces was with the angel praising God. They said, "Glory to God in heaven, and on earth peace among those whom he favors."

Written during the US war with Mexico and the period of unrest that would ultimately explode into the US Civil War, this carol imagines a coming day of peace. Edmund Sears was a pastor and outspoken abolitionist. His social conscience shines through in stanzas 3 and 4, which are sometimes omitted from modern hymnals. Even when contemporary concerns are on the mind of an author, hymnal editors, congregations, or denominations sometimes prefer to stick to beautiful and comfortable versions of the Christmas story.

The text has sometimes been criticized because it does not explicitly mention the birth of Jesus, but its context and exploration of peace on earth is clearly rooted in the nativity narrative and biblical prophecy. Sears was clear-eyed about the "two thousand years of wrong," and his vision of peace as the world returning an echo of the angelic song remains pertinent nearly two centuries after its writing.

REFLECT

Whom do you think the author had in mind in the opening lines of stanza 4? Whom do you picture in your own context?

RESPOND

Use your hymnal's metrical index or the Hymnary website to locate an alternative common meter double (CMD) tune, and try singing the text with it. (These are texts and tunes that have eight lines per stanza, alternating between eight and six syllables. The meter can also be represented as 8.6.8.6D, with the D standing for "double." As the "common" in its name suggests, this is one of the most typical meters for English-language hymns.)

Can you find a pairing that highlights different elements of the text? (KINGSFOLD would be an effective choice.)

JANUARY 3

Refrain:
Go tell it on the mountain,
over the hills and ev'rywhere;
go tell it on the mountain
that Jesus Christ is born!

While shepherds kept their watching
  o'er silent flocks by night,
behold throughout the heavens
  there shone a holy light. *Refrain*

The shepherds feared and trembled
  when lo! above the earth
rang out the angel chorus
  that hailed our Savior's birth. *Refrain*

Down in a lowly manger
  the humble Christ was born,
and God sent us salvation
  that blessed Christmas morn. *Refrain*

African American spiritual; verses by John W. Work Jr. (1871–1925, USA).
Voices Together 252, *Glory to God* 136, *Evangelical Lutheran Worship* 290, *Gather IV* 473

LUKE 2:15–20

When the angels returned to heaven, the shepherds said to each other, "Let's go right now to Bethlehem and see what's happened. Let's confirm what the Lord has revealed to us." They went quickly and found Mary and Joseph, and the baby lying in the manger. When they saw this, they reported what they had been told about this child. Everyone who heard it was amazed at what the shepherds told them. Mary committed these things to memory and considered them carefully. The shepherds returned home, glorifying and praising God for all they had heard and seen. Everything happened just as they had been told.

John W. Work Jr. was a professor at Fisk University, a historically Black institution in Nashville, Tennessee. For several years he directed the Fisk Jubilee Singers, a choir that has played a key role in the preservation and propagation of spirituals around the world since 1871. Their early approach was to adapt songs from aural traditions to satisfy the expectations of audiences versed in European classical music traditions. By doing so they were able to tour internationally and cultivate interest in spirituals, although perhaps at the cost of suggesting that European choral styles were more refined than folk traditions, and, therefore, worthy of concert performance. (I am critiquing not this style of presentation and performance, but rather of the systems of supremacy that created such expectations.)

This song is a rare instance in which the authorship of a spiritual can be at least partially determined. John Work Jr. and his brother Frederick compiled many songs for the Jubilee Singers. The refrain for this one was well-known at the time, but the brothers could not locate words for the verses. (Earlier versions of the text have since been identified and can be found online.) John Work Jr. wrote three new verses to carry forward the Christmas theme of the refrain. His version is now almost universally used.

REFLECT

A number of texts included in this book begin with an imperative word: *come*, *let*, *hark*, and so on. Some are addressed to those of us singing, and some are addressed to God or Christ. How is the command "go" in this text different?

Not only does John Work Jr. artfully continue the Christmas theme through the verses, he presents a contrast between the heights of the "mountain" and the lowliness of Jesus' birth. What other contrasts between high and low appear in the text?

RESPOND

Write a short sending blessing (a benediction) for worship that echoes this hymn.

JANUARY 4

Hark! the herald angels sing,
"Glory to the newborn King!
Peace on earth and mercy mild,
God and sinners reconciled."
Joyful, all ye nations, rise,
join the triumph of the skies.
With th'angelic host proclaim,
"Christ is born in Bethlehem!"

Refrain:
Hark! the herald angels sing,
"Glory to the newborn King!"

Christ, by highest heav'n adored;
Christ, the everlasting Lord,
late in time behold him come,
offspring of the virgin's womb.
Veiled in flesh the Godhead see,
hail th'incarnate deity;
pleased with us in flesh to dwell,
Jesus, our Immanuel! *Refrain*

Hail the heav'n-born Prince of Peace!
Hail the Sun of righteousness!
Light and life to all he brings,
ris'n with healing in his wings.
Mild he lays his glory by,
born that we no more may die,
born to raise us from the earth,
born to give us second birth. *Refrain*

Charles Wesley (1701–1788, England), *Hymns and Sacred Poems*, 1739, alt.
Voices Together 247, *Glory to God* 119, *Evangelical Lutheran Worship* 270, *Gather IV* 475

PHILIPPIANS 2:6–8

Though he was in the form of God,
    he did not consider being equal with God something to exploit.
But he emptied himself
    by taking the form of a slave
    and by becoming like human beings.
When he found himself in the form of a human,
    he humbled himself by becoming obedient to the point of death,
    even death on a cross.

With this Charles Wesley text, we move from an emphasis on the nativity narrative in its various forms to a profound theological meditation on the incarnation. Wesley's text originally began "Hark how all the welkin rings," with *welkin* meaning the vault of heaven, or sky. Each stanza exuberantly celebrates the nature of Christ. It is replete with regal language like King and Lord, but Wesley contrasts the glory of the cosmic Christ with the humility of the incarnation. In doing so he echoes the Philippians 2 passage. "Mild he lays his glory by" is an expression of *kenosis*, a Greek term that means "self-emptying." Though it may sound like a vacuum feature, it refers to Jesus' incarnation and his abandonment of infinite power in favor of finite humanity. ("Pleased with us in flesh to dwell . . .") That the Creator should become one with creation is mind-boggling, but our theologizing about what Jesus gave up in order to become human may miss something of what he reveals about God's nature.

We often ascribe to God characteristics that we most crave for ourselves, making those defining attributes. We desire a God who is all-powerful, all-knowing, and everywhere all at once. But in Jesus we experience a God not defined by might, but rather one who suffered, who learned and grew, and who was imminently present in one time and place. God as encountered in the incarnation—the God who took on flesh and lived among us—is a full revelation of God's character. Being born humble and poor "that we no more may die" is not an exception to God's character; rather, it is fundamental to God's nature. Perhaps these are the attributes of God that we should focus on.

Even so, this scripture and song are both ultimately triumphant in tone—the "incarnate deity" is worthy of praise. And as we will see in tomorrow's continuation of the Philippians passage, all of creation will ultimately respond in worship.

REFLECT

What stands out to you when reading this hymn as a poem (as opposed to singing it)? Do certain words, phrases, or ideas come across differently?

RESPOND

Using a variety of colors (with markers, crayons, colored pencils, or paint), illustrate the angelic choir. Be as abstract as you would like. What colors, shapes, or gestures convey the feeling of their proclamation?

JANUARY 5

Creator of the stars of night,
your people's everlasting light,
O Christ, redeemer of us all,
we pray you hear us when we call.

In sorrow that the ancient curse
should doom to death a universe,
you came, O Savior, to set free
your own in glorious liberty.

When this old world drew on t'ward night,
you came, but not in splendor bright,
not as a monarch, but the child
of Mary, blessed mother mild.

At your great name, O Jesus, now
all knees must bend, all hearts must bow.
All things on earth with one accord,
like those in heav'n, shall call you Lord.

Come in your holy might, we pray,
redeem us for eternal day.
Defend us while we dwell below
from all assaults of our dread foe.

To God Creator, God the Son,
and God the Spirit, Three in One,
praise, honor, might, and glory be
from age to age eternally.

Conditor alme siderum, 9th c.; trans. John Mason Neale (1818–1866, England), 1851, rev. *The Hymnal*, 1940, alt.,

Voices Together 236, *Glory to God* 84, *Evangelical Lutheran Worship* 245, *Gather IV* 458

PHILIPPIANS 2:9–11

Therefore, God highly honored him
        and gave him a name above all names,
    so that at the name of Jesus everyone
        in heaven, on earth, and under the earth might bow
        and every tongue confess
            that Jesus Christ is Lord, to the glory of God the Father.

Like "Hark! the Herald Angels Sing" (see yesterday's entry) but written about eight hundred years earlier, this chant reflects on the nature of Christ. We sing of the one who created the "stars of night" now becoming a part of that very creation. The third stanza connects with the first, even repeating a rhyming "night." In the first stanza, Christ is identified as "everlasting light," but in the third, situated again in the "night," Christ comes "not in splendor bright." Instead, he arrives in humility as the child of Mary.

The hymn goes on to directly paraphrase the Philippians passage. This scripture text is also part of a song, making it one of the oldest Christian hymns. Compare the stanza beginning "At your great name . . ." to the portion of the scripture that starts with "So at the name of Jesus . . ." This is creation's reaction to receiving its Creator: everyone bowing down in worship. The hymn connects the concept of "those in heaven" as well as on earth to the prayer Jesus taught, where we ask that God's "will be done in earth, as it is in heaven" (Matthew 6:10 KJV). Perhaps because it includes everyone on earth, in heaven, and under the earth we can understand it to mean all of creation, fulfilling the vision in Isaiah 11 of all creatures worshiping together.

REFLECT

Despite the song text's emphasis on Christ coming "not as a monarch," it goes on to ask him to come in "holy might." What does this "holy might" mean in light of what we know of Jesus?

RESPOND

Stars are an important image during this season. Draw several in different styles. Try one using only straight lines and another using only curves. Sketch one without lifting your drawing implement from the page.

EPIPHANY

See whose glory fills the skies: Jesus, the light of the world!
Sun of righteousness, arise: Jesus, the light of the world!

Refrain:
We'll walk in the light! Beautiful light!
Shine where the dewdrops of mercy shine bright.
Oh, shine all around us by day and by night,
Jesus, the light of the world.

Pierce the gloom of sin and grief, Jesus, the light of the world!
Scatter all my unbelief, Jesus, the light of the world! *Refrain*

More and more thyself display, Jesus, the light of the world!
Shining to the perfect day, Jesus, the light of the world! *Refrain*

Visit, then, this soul of mine, Jesus, the light of the world!
Fill me, Radiancy divine! Jesus, the light of the world! *Refrain*

Adapt. from Charles Wesley (1707–1788, England), "Christ, Whose Glory Fills the Skies," *Hymns and Sacred Poems*, 1740; additional text and refrain George D. Elderkin (1845–1928, USA), 1890.

Voices Together 274; this tune and refrain paired with "Hark! the Herald Angels Sing," *Glory to God* 127, *All Creation Sings* 914, *Gather IV* 503

JOHN 1:9–14

The true light that shines on all people
    was coming into the world.
The light was in the world,
    and the world came into being through the light,
        but the world didn't recognize the light.
The light came to his own people,
    and his own people didn't welcome him.
But those who did welcome him,
        those who believed in his name,
    he authorized to become God's children,
        born not from blood
        nor from human desire or passion,
        but born from God.
The Word became flesh
    and made his home among us.
    glory like that of a father's only son,
        full of grace and truth.

The last song in our journey from Advent to Epiphany encapsulates what we have been singing from the very beginning—Jesus, Emmanuel, is here—not only in a brief period of history in ancient Palestine, but as the "light of the world" now and forever.

The text originally used for this gospel song tune was "Hark! the Herald Angels Sing" (see entry for January 4), also by Charles Wesley. When assembling the *Voices Together* hymnal, our team spotted the potential to link the tune with "Christ, Whose Glory Fills the Skies" instead. It worked beautifully with the refrain and additional text by composer George Elderkin. The song offers an invitation to not just *feel* or *see* the light of Christ dawning, but to *walk in the light*, the "true light that shines on all people" (John 1:9). May this hymnological journey through familiar and new songs equip you to walk in the light throughout this coming year.

REFLECT

What common themes have emerged for you through this series of songs?

How has this journey through new and familiar hymns affected the way you encounter songs in worship? Do you experience them differently?

How do you hope to "walk in the light" in the coming year?

RESPOND

Find a way to respond creatively to songs you encounter in worship in the future. If your church uses a hymnal, consider purchasing your own copy and using it to make marginal notes or sketches. Or make yourself a song journal to record your responses to worship. Consider choosing a few songs used in your church's Sunday gathering to reflect on throughout the week.

ACKNOWLEDGMENTS

I am grateful for the communities that have infused me with the songs of the church from an early age until today, including those I have served in various capacities:

Oak Grove Mennonite Church, Grantsville, Maryland
Auburn Christian Fellowship, Auburn, Alabama
First Baptist Church, Corvallis, Oregon
Belmont Mennonite Church, Elkhart, Indiana
Bethel Missionary Church, Goshen, Indiana
Waterford Mennonite Church, Goshen, Indiana
College Mennonite Church, Goshen, Indiana
Calvary United Methodist Church, Elkhart, Indiana
Hyattsville Mennonite Church, Hyattsville, Maryland
Prairie Street Mennonite Church, Elkhart, Indiana
Faith Mennonite Church, Goshen, Indiana

I would like to thank those who read an earlier draft of this material and provided helpful feedback:

SaeJin Lee, a valued colleague from the *Voices Together* committee, who provided an artist's perspective to the response prompts.

Carl P. Daw Jr., my mentor and teacher in hymn writing for over twenty years and author of material in this book, who offered hymnological fact-checking.

María Tice, my spouse, who regularly helps me clarify my writing; dear reader, you have her to thank for a substantial reduction in semicolons in this book.

And finally, my deepest gratitude to Sara Versluis, my editor at Herald Press. As an editor myself, I especially appreciate the depth of wisdom and patience she brought to this project, always prodding me toward deeper engagement with the material and greater quality.

SONG TEXT ACKNOWLEDGMENTS

The publisher gratefully acknowledges permission to reproduce texts and translations granted by publishers, organizations, and individuals listed as copyright holders. Specific acknowledgments for copyrighted works are listed in alphabetical order; information is also reproduced alongside each text in the devotional entries.

"Bless'd be the God of Israel" by Michael A. Perry © 1973 The Jubilate Group

"Come, Join in Mary's Prophet-Song" by Adam M. L. Tice © 2009 GIA Publications, Inc.

"Come Now, O God," by David Bjorlin © 2017 GIA Publications, Inc.

"Creator of the Stars of Night" translation by John Mason Neale © 1985 The Church Pension Fund

"From Heaven Above to Earth I Come" translation by Catherine Winkworth, *Lyra Germanica*, Series 1, 1855, composite translation Inter-Lutheran Commission on Worship, alt., © 1978 *Lutheran Book of Worship* (admin. Augsburg Fortress)

"From the Parent's Heart, the Firstborn (Corde natus exparentis)" translation by Carl P. Daw © 2019 Hope Publishing Co., Carol Stream, IL 60188; All rights reserved.

"Hacia Belén (Alegría) (Mary Journeyed)" English translation by Mary Louise Bringle © 2005 GIA Publications, Inc.

"Hope Is a Candle" by Richard Leach © 1995 Selah Publishing Co., Inc.

"In the Beginning" by Chris Shelton © 2015 GIA Publications, Inc.

"Jesus Entered Egypt" by Adam M. L. Tice © 2009 GIA Publications, Inc.

"My Soul Cries Out / Canticle of the Turning" by Rory Cooney © 1990 GIA Publications, Inc.

"Now the Heavens Start to Whisper" by Mary Louise Bringle © 2006 GIA Publications, Inc.

"Poor of the Earth" by Jacque B. Jones © 2014 GIA Publications, Inc.

"Prepare the Way! the Prophet Called" by David Gambrell © 2015 GIA Publications, Inc.

"Sleepers, Wake" stanza 1 translation by Carl P. Daw © 1982 Hope Publishing Company, Carol Stream, IL 60188; All rights reserved.

"Unexpected and Mysterious" by Jeannette M. Lindholm © 2002 Jeannette M. Lindholm (admin. Augsburg Fortress.)

"We Dream of a Turning," by Adam M. L. Tice, © 2009 GIA Publications, Inc.

SONG TITLE INDEX

SCRIPTURE INDEX

THE AUTHOR

Adam M. L. Tice is a hymn and songwriter and the text editor for the *Voices Together* hymnal. His texts appear in many recent hymnals and supplements worldwide, as well as in numerous choral settings. He has written nearly three hundred hymns published in five collections, as well as on GIA's online congregational song platform, Unbound. In 2024, Tice was named a Fellow of the Hymn Society and also received Goshen College's Culture for Service alumni award.

Tice currently works as editor for congregational song with GIA Publications. He has an MA in Christian formation with an emphasis on worship from Anabaptist Mennonite Biblical Seminary. He is ordained for ministry in Mennonite Church USA, and he regularly leads workshops, presentations, and singing at conferences and events locally and nationally. In his leisure time, Tice enjoys rock climbing. Due to the geographical constraints of Indiana, he generally climbs indoors. He is a volunteer route setter at his local gym. He lives in Goshen, Indiana, with his spouse, María. They are recent empty nesters as their only child, Ezra, began college in 2026.

Tice's hymn collections and other work include:

Woven into Harmony, 2009
A Greener Place to Grow, 2011
Stars Like Grace, 2013
Claim the Mystery, 2015
Pulse and Breath, 2019
Recording: *Walk in Peace: The Songs of Sally Ann Morris and Adam M. L. Tice*
Come, Walk with Us: Songs of Justice for All Ages, edited by Anneli Loepp Thiessen and Adam M. L. Tice; illustrated by Haeon Grace Kang

Advent devotionals from Herald Press

Carols for the Coming Christ
A Daily Devotional from Advent to Epiphany
by Adam M. L. Tice

Comfort and Joy
Readings and Practices for Advent
by Sherah-Leigh Gerber and Gwen Lantz

Expecting Emmanuel
Eight Women Who Prepared the Way
by Joanna Harader

The Holy in the Night
Finding Freedom in a Season of Waiting
by Shannon W. Dycus

Unhappy Holidays
Blessings for a Blue Christmas
by Sherah-Leigh Gerber